italian
grammar

Anna Proudfoot

TEACH YOURSELF BOOKS

For UK order queries: please contact Bookpoint Ltd, 78 Milton Park, Abingdon, Oxon
OX14 4TD. Telephone: (44) 01235 400414, Fax: (44) 01235 400454. Lines are open from
9.00–6.00, Monday to Saturday, with a 24 hour message answering service.
Email address: orders@bookpoint.co.uk

For U.S.A. & Canada order queries: please contact NTC/Contemporary Publishing,
4255 West Touhy Avenue, Lincolnwood, Illinois 60646–1975, U.S.A.
Telephone: (847) 679 5500, Fax: (847) 679 2494.

Long renowned as the authoritative source for self-guided learning – with more than
30 million copies sold worldwide – the *Teach Yourself* series includes over 200 titles in
the fields of languages, crafts, hobbies, business and education.

British Library Cataloguing in Publication Data
A catalogue record for this title is available from The British Library.

Library of Congress Catalog Card Number: On file

First published in UK 2000 by Hodder Headline Plc, 338 Euston Road, London, NW1 3BH.

First published in US 2000 by NTC/Contemporary Publishing, 4255 West Touhy Avenue,
Lincolnwood (Chicago), Illinois 60646–1975 U.S.A.

Typeset by Transet Limited, Coventry, England.
Printed in Great Britain for Hodder & Stoughton Educational, a division of Hodder
Headline Plc, 338 Euston Road, London NW1 3BH by Cox & Wyman Ltd, Reading,
Berkshire.

Impression number   10 9 8 7 6 5 4 3 2 1
Year   2006 2005 2004 2003 2002 2001 2000

CONTENTS

Functional grammar Units 1–22

1 Asking for and giving personal information

Say who you are, what your name is ■ Say where
you are from, what nationality you are ■ Say what
region or city you are from ■ Say what your occupation and
marital status is ■ Ask other people for similar
information ■ Give similar information about

2 Identifying people and things

Ask for something ■ Ask or say what something is
■ Ask or say who someone is ■ Indicate or point out

3 Asking about availability

Ask and say if something or someone exists ■ Say where
something is ■ Ask and say if something is available

4 Talking about location

Ask where something or someone is ■ Say where

5 Stating choice and preference

Ask the cost of a thing or things ■ Express a preference
■ Specify which item you want ■ Use numbers ■

1 Nouns with irregular plurals

1.1 Invariable nouns
1.2 Irregular plural forms

2 Adjectives extra

2.1 *bello, buono, grande, santo*

3 Comparison

3.1 Comparative adjectives
3.2 Relationship of equality: adjectives
3.3 Superlative adjectives
3.4 Comparative adverbs
3.5 Relationship of equality: adverbs
3.6 Superlative adverbs

4 Pronouns

5 Indefinites

6 Quantity

7 Relative pronouns

8 Prepositions

9 Negatives

10 Question words

11 Conjunctions

12 Linking parts of sentences

INTRODUCTION

This fully revised edition is designed as a reference guide for all those studying Italian on their own or in a class, and particularly for those using textbooks written along communicative lines, who feel they need some grammar back-up. You do not need a specialised knowledge of grammar terms in order to use this book, because everything is explained in a non-technical way. There is also a short glossary of grammatical terms.

The book is suitable for all levels from complete beginners to A-level and even beyond. It is designed for the independent user, but can also be used as back-up in a class situation. It is particularly helpful in that it explains grammar points in English, since many students find it hard to follow explanations in textbooks written entirely in Italian.

The book is divided into units, each one covering a basic communicative function, such as 'Asking for and giving personal information', 'Talking about location', 'Describing the past'. In each unit you will find the constructions you need to carry out the particular language function covered, along with the essential vocabulary and important grammar points. You will also find language exercises which allow you to practise the points learned.

For each unit, the contents pages list both the language functions and the grammar points covered, so that you can see at a glance what is included. If, on the other hand, you want to check specific grammar points, look up the index at the back of the book.

ABOUT THE AUTHOR

Anna Proudfoot was born in Scotland but has spent long periods in Italy since childhood. Since graduating from the University of London, she has taught Italian in higher, further and adult education in London, Cambridge, the USA and now Oxford. Her main interests are in developing language materials for adult learners and she has written three Italian Grammar textbooks. She is currently Head of Italian at Oxford Brookes University, where she is also in charge of Oxford Brookes Languages Services, which offers language training for business and runs intensive Italian language weekends for the general public.

HOW TO USE
THIS BOOK

Each of the units in this book is free-standing so if you want to learn or revise all your Italian grammar, you can work through the units in any order you like. If there is a particular language function that you need to use, you can check the contents pages to find out which unit deals with the function that interests you. Unit 16, for example, teaches you how to express your likes and dislikes, unit 7 shows you how to talk about your daily routine.

Start by reading the **Learn how to** box which lists the language functions studied in the unit. The section **Language points** tells you which grammar constructions you are going to need in order to carry out those functions. The **Introduction** gives a few examples (with English translation) of these constructions, along with a very brief explanation. When you have looked at these examples, you are ready to study the **Focus on grammar**, in which all the grammar points are dealt with one by one. Detailed explanations are illustrated by examples.

Once you feel confident about using the language points you have just learnt, you can expand your knowledge by reading the section **Language Plus**. This section gives alternative ways of expressing the functions you have been studying, and mentions additional language points.

The **Language in Action** section at the end of each unit shows you how these language functions are used in the context of everyday life and gives you practical exercises to do on each point, with examples taken from both spoken language and written language.

Any grammar points not covered directly in the units will be found in the **Grammar Appendix**, along with a list of common verbs and their links, and a list of the most common irregular verbs.

The **Index** lists specific grammar points as well as key words in alphabetical order.

GLOSSARY

active construction – all verbs that take an object can either have an *active* form – *lasciamo* **la macchina nel garage** *(we leave the car in the garage)* – or a *passive* form – **la macchina** *viene lasciata* **nel garage** *(the car is left in the garage)*. An active construction is one in which the subject of the sentence is the person carrying out the action, as in the first example. *(See also passive)*.

adjective – gives information about a noun. The biggest group of adjectives is that of descriptive adjectives, used to describe objects or people: e.g., size, colour, shape, nationality. Other adjectives can be found under separate categories: see *demonstrative, indefinite, interrogative* and *possessive*.

adverb – gives information about a verb, saying how, when or where something is done. Adverbs such as **molto, poco, tanto** can also add further information about an adjective or another adverb.

agreement – in Italian, adjectives, articles and sometimes past participles have to 'agree with' the noun or pronoun they refer to, in number and gender. This means that their form varies according to whether the noun/pronoun is masculine or feminine, singular or plural.

article – Italian has two main types: the definite article **il, lo**, etc. *(the)* and the indefinite article **un, una**, etc. *(a)*. The partitive **dei, delle, degli**, etc. *(some, any)* is also considered an article.

auxiliary verbs – such as **avere** and **essere** used with the past participle to form compound tenses, both active *ho* **mangiato** *(I have eaten)*, *siamo* **entrati** *(we went in)* and passive *è stato* **ammazzato** *(he was killed)*. (See also *modal auxiliary*).

clause – a part of a sentence which contains a subject and a verb. Complex sentences are made up of a series of clauses. The main clause is the part which makes sense on its own and does not depend on any other element in the sentence. A subordinate clause always depends on another clause, and is often introduced by a conjunction such as **che**. Subordinate clauses include time clauses, relative clauses, purpose clauses, result clauses, conditional clauses, clauses of exception.

comparative – used to compare one element with another, whether person, object or activity. Specifically, there are comparative adjectives and comparative adverbs.

compound tenses – formed by the auxiliary **avere** or **essere**, and the past participle. They include the perfect (*passato prossimo*), pluperfect (*trapassato*), past conditional, future perfect, and, of course, the passive tenses.

conditional – not a tense, but a verb mood. It can be used on its own, particularly as a polite way of expressing a request, or in conditional sentences, where the statement contained in the main clause is dependent on some condition being met.

conjugation – the pattern according to which verb forms change according to the person, tense or mood. It also means the actual groups of verbs ending in **-are, -ere, -ire** to which regular verbs belong.

conjunction – a 'joining' word, usually linking two words, phrases or clauses within a sentence. It can be as simple as **e** *(and)* or **ma** *(but)*, or more complex. Specific conjunctions include those beginning clauses of condition, result, purpose, exception. Many of these require the use of subjunctive. (See *subordinate clause*).

countable – a noun is countable if it can normally be used in both singular and plural, and take the indefinite article **un, una**, etc. An uncountable noun is one which does not normally have a plural, e.g., **latte** *(milk)*, or an abstract noun such as **coraggio** *(courage)*.

definite article: see *article*

demonstrative – a demonstrative adjective or a pronoun is one which demonstrates or indicates the person or object referred to: the most common ones in Italian are **questo** and **quello**.

direct object – whether noun or pronoun, it is something or someone directly affected by the action or event. It is always used with a *transitive* verb.

feminine – see *gender*

gender – all nouns in Italian have a gender: they are either masculine or feminine, even if they are inanimate objects. Grammatical gender is not always a guide to natural gender: e.g., **giraffa** is female in gender but is used for a male or female giraffe. Gender is important since it determines the form of noun, article and adjective and even past participle.

gerund – a verb form ending in **-ando** or **-endo**: **parlando** *(speaking)*, **sorridendo** *(smiling)*, **finendo** *(finishing)*. The gerund can be used with the verb **stare** to express a continuous action or event: *sto mangiando (I'm just eating)*.

idiomatic – an idiomatic expression is one which cannot normally be translated literally, for example **sono morta di sonno** *(I'm dead tired)*.

imperative – the verb mood used to express orders, commands or instructions.

impersonal (verbs, verb forms) – such as **basta** *(it is enough)*, **occorre** *(it is necessary)* do not refer to one particular person. They can generally be translated by English *it* and a third person form. These verbs can be personalised by adding a personal pronoun, usually the indirect object: e.g., **mi basta sapere questo**. *(I only need to know this)*.

indefinite article – see *article*

indefinite – an adjective or pronoun used to refer to a person or thing in a general way, rather than a definite person or thing. Examples are: **alcuni** *(some)*, **certi** *(certain, some)*, **qualche** *(some)*.

indicative (verb) – the verb mood we use most of the time. It has a full range of tenses: present, past, future. (See also *subjunctive*).

indirect object – an object, whether noun or pronoun, that is indirectly affected by the action or event. An indirect object can be found in the same sentence as a direct object: **ho mandato delle cartoline** (direct) *ai miei amici* (indirect) *(I sent some postcards to my friends)*. It can also be used with an intransitive verb, with a preposition such as **a**, **da**: e.g., **Marco telefonava al suo amico ogni sera** *(Marco used to phone his friend every evening)*.

infinitive – the form in which a verb is listed in dictionaries recognised by its endings **-are**, **-ere**, **-ire**. It cannot be used on its own but depends on a verb, often a *modal verb*: **vorrei** *ringraziare* **i collaboratori** *(I would like to thank my collaborators)* or following a *preposition*: **siamo andati in centro per** *comprare* **i biglietti** *(we took a trip into town to buy the tickets)*.

interrogative – a word which is used to ask a question or an indirect question. These include **chi** *(who)*, **come** *(how)*, **cosa** *(what)*, **dove** *(where)*, **quale** *(which)*, **quando** *(when)*, **perché** *(why)*.

intransitive (verb) – a verb which cannot be used with a direct object. Some can be used with an indirect object, e.g., **telefonare a**. Some are used without any object, e.g., verbs of movement. Many of these verbs take the auxiliary **essere**, but not all. It is important to remember that sometimes a verb which can be used transitively in English *(to walk the dog)* cannot be used transitively in Italian: **camminare** cannot take an object. Finally, some verbs can be used both transitively and intransitively (See *transitive verb*).

invariable – an invariable noun is one that has the same form for both singular and plural: **un** *film*, **dei** *film* or for both masculine and feminine: **un** *artista*, **un'***artista*. An invariable adjective, e.g., **rosa** *(pink)* is one which does not change its form to agree with the noun, whether masculine or feminine, singular or plural.

irregular (noun or verb) – one which does not follow one of the standard patterns of forms or endings.

masculine – see *gender*

modal verb (modal auxiliary) – a verb which is used with an infinitive, such as **potere** *(to be able to)*, **dovere** *(to have to)*, **volere** *(to want to)*, as in *posso* **lavorare domani** *I can work tomorrow*.

mood – the ways in which verbs can express actions or event. The four main moods – all of which, except the imperative, have a range of tenses – are the *indicative*, *subjunctive*, *conditional* and *imperative*.

negative – words or phrases that turn a positive statement or question into a negative one. Italian uses mainly double negatives, or pairs of negative elements. Examples of negatives include: **nessun** *(no)*, **nessuno** *(nobody)*, **niente** *(nothing)*, **non … mai** *(not ever, never)*, **non … ancora** *(not yet)*, **non … più** *(no longer, no more)*.

noun – indicates a person, place, thing, or event, for example. Nouns are inextricably linked to the articles (**il, un,** etc.) and to any adjectives that accompany them. All nouns have a gender and this determines the form of the adjectives and articles that go with it.

number – the distinction between *singular* and *plural*. Verb forms alter according to the number of the subject: **il ragazzo** *nuota (the boy swims)*, **i ragazzi** *nuotano (the boys swim)*.

object – in grammatical terms, the person or thing affected by the action or event, as opposed to the subject, which is the person or thing responsible for it. (See *direct object*, *indirect object*.)

participle (present, past) – verbs normally have a present participle and a past participle. The past participle is used with the verb **avere** or **essere** to form the *passato prossimo* tense. When used with **essere**, it 'agrees' with the subject: **siamo andati**.

partitive article – see *article*

passive (verb forms) – in a passive construction, the subject of the sentence is the person or thing affected by the action or event taking place: **tutti gli studenti sono stati promossi** *(all the students were moved up a class)*. (See also *active construction*).

person – the verb subject can be a first person (**io** *I*), second person (**tu** *you*) third person (**lui, lei** *he, she*) and so on.

personal pronoun – may be a subject pronoun: **io, tu, lui** *(I, you, he)* etc; direct object pronoun: **mi, ti, lo, la** *(me, you, him, her)* etc; indirect object pronoun: **mi, ti, gli, le** *(to me, to you, to him, to her)* etc; disjunctive pronoun, used as a stressed direct object or after preposition **(con) me, te, lui, lei** *(with) me, you, him, her)* etc. (See also *pronoun*)

plural – see *number*

possessive – possessive adjectives and/or pronouns denote ownership: *il mio* **orologio** *(my watch)*.

preposition – a word which gives further information about a person, action or event, referring, for example, to time or place, value or purpose. Examples include **a, con, da, di, in, per, su**.

pronoun – a word which stands in for and/or refers to a noun. There are various categories of pronoun: demonstrative, indefinite, interrogative, personal, possessive, reflexive, relative.

question – direct questions sometimes begin with a question word: **dove vai stasera?** *(where are you going this evening?)* and sometimes do not **hai fame?** *(are you hungry?)*. Indirect questions are introduced by words such as **chiedere** *(to ask)*.

reflexive verb – a verb that can be used with a reflexive pronoun, equivalent of English *myself, himself*, indicating that the subject and the object are one and the same: **mi lavo** *(I wash)*. Sometimes the verb can only be used reflexively, and no object is actually present, e.g., **vergognarsi** *(to be ashamed)*.

regular – a regular noun or verb is one which follows one of the main noun or verb patterns, whose forms and endings can be predicted: e.g., **-are**, **parlare** *(to speak)*, **-ere**, **sorridere** *(to smile)*, **-ire**, **partire** *(to leave)*.

relative – a relative pronoun introduces a relative clause, which gives more information about a person or thing mentioned or an event referred to: **ho visto la segretaria** *che* **lavorava con Di Martino** *(I saw the secretary who worked with Di Martino)*.

reported speech – also known as indirect speech, a way of relating words spoken or written by someone else. Reported speech is usually introduced by verbs such as **dire** *(to say, to tell)*, **scrivere** *(to write)*, **annunciare** *(to announce)* and the conjunction **che**.

sentence – must have a verb and a subject. It can either be a simple sentence (one subject, one verb): **i bambini dormivano** *(the children were asleep)* or a complex sentence (main clause and one or more subordinate clauses): **mentre i bambini dormivano, i genitori hanno messo in ordine la stanza** *(while the children were asleep, their parents tidied the room)*.

singular – see *number*

stem – see *verb stem*

subject – is usually a noun, (subject) pronoun (**io, tu, lei**, etc.) or proper name denoting the person or object performing the action or the event taking place. In the case of a passive construction, the subject is the person or thing affected by the action. With Italian verbs, it is not always essential to have a subject mentioned since it is understood from the verb form: *abbiamo mangiato* **a mezzogiorno** *(we ate at midday)*.

subjunctive – used to express doubt or uncertainty. It is almost always used in complex sentences where one clause depends on another. (See *subordinate clause*). However, it can also be found standing on its own, when used as an imperative form: *vada* **via!** *(go away!).*

subordinate clause – one that depends on another clause, usually the main clause in a sentence. The subordinate clause may depend on a main verb expressing uncertainty, e.g., **dubitare**, or a conjunction such as **benché**, or a relative pronoun such as **che**. (See also *conjunction*).

superlative – when one or more persons, objects or activities are compared, a superlative form is used to express the one which is superior to all the rest: **la casa di Matilde era** *la più grande* **del paese** *(Mathilde's house was the biggest in the village)*. (See also *comparative*).

tense – a finite verb form that normally provides a clue as to the time setting (present, past, future) for an action or event: **andremo a New York** *(we will go to New York)*.

transitive verb – a verb which can always be used transitively, or in other words with a direct object: *ho fumato* **una sigaretta** *(I smoked a cigarette)*. Sometimes no object is used *ho fumato (I smoked)*, but the verb is still a transitive verb since it can take an object. Some verbs can be used both transitively and intransitively: e.g., **aumentare** *(to increase)*, **diminuire** *(to decrease)*, **cambiare** *(to change)*.

verb – a word that describes an action, event or state. It always has a subject and can also have an object. Its form varies according to mood and tense, and the person, gender and number of its subject.

verb stem – the 'base', or part of the verb which is left when you remove **-are**, **-ere**, **-ire** from the infinitive form. In a regular verb the ending changes but the stem does not normally change. In an irregular verb, the stem may change too.

voice – verbs normally have two voices: *active* and *passive*. (See *active* and *passive*).

1 | ASKING FOR AND GIVING PERSONAL INFORMATION

Learn how to ...

■ Say who you are / what your name is ■ Say where you are from/what nationality you are ■ Say what region or city you are from ■ Say what your occupation and marital status is ■ Ask other people for similar information ■ Give similar information about other people

Language points

■ Subject pronouns **io, tu, lui**, etc. ■ Verb **essere** (present tense) ■ Verb **chiamarsi** (present tense) ■ Adjectives of nationality, region, city of origin ■ Profession, marital status, titles

Introduction

To give or ask for personal information, you need to know the subject pronouns **io, tu, Lei**, etc., *(I, you, etc.),* the verb **chiamarsi** *(to be called),* and the verb **essere** *(to be).* Look at these examples before going on:

Mi chiamo Anna.	*My name's Anna.*
Sono inglese.	*I'm English.*
Sono di Oxford.	*I'm from Oxford.*
Lei è italiana?	*Are you Italian?*
È di Roma?	*Are you from Rome?*
Lui si chiama George. È inglese.	*He's called George. He's English.*
E lei?	*And (what about) her?*
Lei si chiama Georgina. È inglese.	*She's called Georgina. She's English.*

Focus on Grammar

1 Io, tu, lui, lei, Lei

The subject pronouns **io, tu, lui, lei, Lei**, etc. (English *I, you,* etc) are not normally used in Italian, because the ending of the verb shows which person is being talked about. The pronouns can, however, be used for emphasis, for example:

a) when you want to distinguish betwen *he* and *she*, which have the same verb form:

Lui è inglese.	*He is English.*
Lei è italiana.	*She is Italian.*

b) when you want to emphasise a difference or contrast:

Io sono italiana.	*I am Italian (and female!).*
Lui è inglese.	*He is English.*

c) to make a question sound less abrupt, particularly when using the polite form:

Lei è italiana?	*Are you Italian?*

Here are the forms of subject pronouns generally used in this situation:

Singular		Plural	
io	*I*	**noi**	*we*
tu	*you* (*informal*)	**voi**	*you*
lui	*he*	**loro**	*them*
lei	*she*		
Lei	*you* (*formal*)	**Loro**	*you* (*formal*)

2 Tu *or* Lei?

Italian has two forms of address meaning *you* in the singular: **tu** (the informal form) used with friends, family, children and animals; and **Lei** (the formal form, normally written with capital 'L') which is used in business situations, such as a shop or a bank, with new acquaintances (until invited to use **tu**) and with people older than you or worthy of respect. **Lei** uses the same form of the verb as **lui** *(he)* or **lei** *(she).*

There is also a formal form of address for more than one person – **Loro** – which uses the same form of verb as **loro** *(they)* but this is much less common. A waiter, shop assistant or hotel receptionist may use **loro** when addressing more than one client. But it would not be impolite to use the more informal **voi** form.

3 Essere

The verb **essere** *(to be)* is used to give information about yourself, such as where you are from or what nationality you are.

Italian verbs come into three main groups with their infinitive forms ending **-are, -ere,** or **-ire.** Usually they follow a set pattern according to the group they 'belong' to, but **essere** *(to be)* does not follow such a pattern. Here are all the forms of the verb **essere** with the subject pronouns you could use:

	Singular			**Plural**	
(io)	**sono**	*I am*	(noi)	**siamo**	*we are*
(tu)	**sei**	*you are*	(voi)	**siete**	*you are*
(lui)	**è**	*he is*	(loro)	**sono**	*they are*
(lei)	**è**	*she is*			
(Lei)	**è**	*you are (formal)*	(Loro)*	**sono**	*you are (formal)*

*The **Loro** form (formal *you*) is shown here and in the **chiamarsi** table below. It is always the same as the **loro** *(they)* form, so is not shown separately in future units.

4 Chiamarsi

The Italian for 'my name is' is **mi chiamo** (Lit: *I call myself*). To say this, you need the verb **chiamarsi** *(to call oneself).* This is a reflexive verb (see unit 7 for a fuller explanation of these verbs).

	Singular	
(io)	**mi** chiamo	*I am called*
(tu)	**ti** chiami	*you are called*
(lui)	**si** chiama	*he is called*
(lei)	**si** chiama	*she is called*
(Lei)	**si** chiama	*you called* (formal)
	Plural	
(noi)	**ci** chiami**amo**	*we are called*
(voi)	**vi** chiam**ate**	*you are called*
(loro)	**si** chiam**ano**	*they are called*
(Loro)	**si** chiam**ano**	*you are called* (formal form)

Come ti chiami?   **Come si chiama?**

Italians don't say *What are you called?* but *How are you called*?

For more verbs that end in **-are** (**mangiare, parlare** etc) see units 5 and 6. For more reflexive verbs (actions you do to or for yourself and which require reflexive pronouns) see unit 7.

5 Nationality and other adjectives

An adjective tells you about someone or something. Use it with the verb **essere** to say what nationality someone is:

Sara **è** italiana.   *Sara is Italian.*

In Italian, the adjective has to agree with the person (or object) it describes, i.e. it must have a masculine or feminine, singular or plural ending to match the person (people) or thing (things) it is describing. In Italian, objects – like people – are either masculine or feminine, singular or plural. For further notes on agreement, see unit 2.

There are two main types of adjective in Italian:

a) Those ending in **-e** (same for masculine or feminine) whose plural ends in **-i**:

Henry è ingles**e**.   *Henry is English.*
Henrietta è ingles**e**.   *Henrietta is English.*
Henry e Henrietta sono ingles**i**.   *Henry and Henrietta are English.*

b) Those ending in **-o** (masculine) or **-a** (feminine) whose plural is **-i** (masculine) or **-e** (feminine):

Mario è italian**o**.	*Mario is Italian.*
Maria è italian**a**.	*Maria is Italian.*
Mario e Piero sono italian**i**.	*Mario and Piero are Italian (men).*
Maria e Teresa sono italian**e**.	*Maria and Teresa are Italian (women).*
Mario e Maria sono italian**i**.	*Mario and Maria are Italian (one man, one woman).*

The last example shows how, when there is one male and one female subject, the adjective becomes masculine for both of them!

6 Town or Region

Just as important as nationality is which region of Italy a person comes from. Italians are very loyal to their town, city or village. So the following questions and answers might be heard:

Di dove sei?	*Where are you from?*
Sono di Bari. E tu?	*I'm from Bari. And you?*
Io sono milanese (di Milano).	*I'm from Milan.*
Mia madre è pugliese però.	*My mother is from Puglia however.*

7 Titles

Titles are important in Italy as an acknowledgement of someone's professional status. Specific titles are used for an engineer (**ingegnere**), lawyer (**avvocato**), accountant (**ragioniere**), lecturer or secondary school teacher (**professore, professoressa**), doctor or even just graduate (**dottore, dottoressa**). You can also use just **signore** or **signora** (**signorina** is used only for young girls) but it is very common, particularly in the south, for all men of any status to be addressed as **dottore**. Before a surname, a final 'e' is dropped from titles:

Buongiorno, Avvocato.	Buona notte, Dottore.
Buongiorno, Avvocato Bruni!	Buona notte, Dottor Esposito!
Buonasera, Ingegnere.	
Buonasera, Ingegner Bianchi!	

Language plus

1 Profession or occupation

You can extend a conversation by asking someone his or her profession or occupation:

Lei è professore?   *Are you a teacher?*
No. Sono medico. E Lei?   *No. I'm a doctor. What about you?*
Io sono avvocato.   *I'm a lawyer.*

Notes:

- **Un, una** (*a*) are sometimes omitted when saying what you do or asking someone about their occupation.

- Some nouns denoting professions have distinct forms for men and for women:

Masculine	Feminine		Masculine	Feminine	
maestro	maestra	*teacher*	professore	professoressa	*lecturer,*
sarto	sarta	*tailor,*			*teacher*
		dressmaker	dottore	dottoressa	*doctor,*
cuoco	cuoca	*cook*			*graduate*
infermiere	infermiera	*nurse*	studente	studentessa	*student*
cameriere	cameriera	*waiter,*	attore	attrice	*actor*
		waitress	scrittore	scrittrice	*writer*
ragioniere	ragioniera	*accountant*	direttore	direttrice	*manager*

- Other nouns denoting occupations have the same ending, for both sexes. For men these nouns use the article **un** or **uno**; for women **una** or **un'**: e.g., **un dentista** (male), **una dentista** (female).

-e	cantante	*singer*		
	insegnante	*teacher*		
-ista	dentista	*dentist*	turista	*tourist*
	artista	*artist*	pianista	*pianist*
	autista	*driver*	ciclista	*cyclist*
	giornalista	*journalist*		

■ Lastly, for some professions, it doesn't make any difference whether you are male or female. The masculine version is used for both with the masculine article: e.g., **(un) medico** *(doctor)*, **(un) avvocato** *(lawyer)* and **(un) vigile** *(traffic warden)*.

Carlo/Carla è medico.

Use of the female forms **avvocatessa**, **vigilessa** is considered condescending.

2 Marital status

The verb **essere** is used also to give information about marital status:

Giovanni **è** sposato.	*Giovanni is married.*
Maria **è** sposata.	*Maria is married.*
Giovanni e Maria **sono** sposati.	*Giovanni and Maria are married.*

Although the terms **celibe** *(bachelor)* and **nubile** *(spinster)* exist, Italians prefer to say:

Non è sposato.	*He isn't married.*
Non è sposata.	*She isn't married.*

3 Asking questions

A statement can be turned into a question in two different ways:

a) Change the order, putting the subject (**tu, Lei**) after the verb:

Statement:	Lei è inglese.
Question:	È inglese Lei?

b) Raise the intonation of the voice at the end of the sentence:

Lei è inglese?

4 Negative sentences

Negative sentences (statements or questions) are formed simply by adding **non** immediately before the verb:

Sono inglese.	*I'm English.*
Non sono inglese.	*I'm not English.*
Sei studente?	*Are you a student?*
Non sei studente?	*Aren't you a student?*

Lei è italiana?   *Are you Italian?*
Lei **non** è italiana?   *Aren't you Italian?*

It's not difficult to say *no*!

Sei italiana?
No, non sono italiana.

Language in action

Exercise 1

Note and learn how people introduce themselves in the first three scenes and then try to complete the conversation in Scene 4.

1 *Al lavoro*

In this scene, where Simon is being introduced to his new colleagues at the **Città d'Acqua** offices in Venice, the **Lei** form is used, because people are meeting for the first time. Otherwise in a work situation, colleagues may use **tu**. '**Questo**' is used to indicate the person being introduced (see unit 2).

Mara, questo è Simon, lo   *Mara, this is Simon, the*
  studente inglese.   *English student.*
Simon, questa è Bruna, la mia   *Simon, this is Bruna, my*
  collega.   *colleague.*
Piacere, Bruna.   *Pleased to meet you, Bruna.*
Anche Lei è di Venezia?   *Are you from Venice too?*
No. Sono francese, di Nizza.   *No. I'm French, from Nice.*
  E tu?   *And you?*
Io sono di Londra.   *I'm from London.*

2 *Ad un ricevimento*

At a drinks party, you might introduce yourself to someone, again using the **Lei** form to ask their name:

Io sono Marco Baralle, della ditta *I'm Marco Baralle, of Baralle*
  Baralle e Carpaldi. Lei come   *and Carpaldi. What's*
  si chiama?   *your name?*
Mi chiamo Cristina Caria. Sono   *My name's Cristina Caria.*
  una collega di Gianni Prestini.   *I'm a colleague of Gianni Prestini.*

3 Ad una festa di studenti

Children or younger people starting up a conversation will probably address each other informally, using the **tu** form, right from the start.

Ciao, come ti chiami?
Io sono Marina. E tu?
Mi chiamo Filippo. E questa è mia sorella, Chiara.
Ciao, Chiara.
Ciao.

4 Al bar

Now complete the conversation in this scene. Choose from among the options **la mia amica inglese / uno studente inglese / un turista tedesco**.

Ciao, Valentina. Questa è Mary, ...
Ciao, Mary. Io sono Daniela, questo è Hans.
Piacere. Io sono Hans, sono .... di Monaco di Baviera.
Scusa, Valentina, il tuo ragazzo come si chiama?
Io sono James, ...

Exercise 2

Choose one of the characters described below and imagine you are introducing yourself as him or her. Using the information given, tell someone your name, nationality and occupation.

1.

| Tracy Jones |
| Milton Keynes |
| Student |
| English |

3.

| Dr. Joe Barnes |
| Oxford |
| Lecturer |
| Welsh |

2.

| Massimiliano Lusardi |
| Genova |
| Student |
| Italian |

4.

| Camilla Pennino |
| Roma |
| Doctor |
| Italian |

Exercise 3

americano	austriaco	gallese	inglese	irlandese
	italiano	scozzese	tedesco	

Di che nazionalità sono?

e.g. Pierre-Philippe è di Bayeux. È *francese.*

1 Heinz è di Mainz. È ....

2 Blodwen è di Llangollen. È ....

3 Callum e Malcolm sono di Aberdeen. Sono ....

4 Padraig è di Laoghaire. È ....

5 Maria Teresa e Aldo sono di Genova. Sono ....

6 Oswald e Mathilde sono di Vienna. Sono ....

7 Jim e Mary-Jo sono di New Orleans. Sono ....

8 Charlotte e Sophie sono di Chobham, Surrey. Sono ....

2 | IDENTIFYING PEOPLE AND THINGS

Learn how to ...

■ Ask for something ■ Ask or say what something is ■ Ask or say who someone is ■ Indicate or point out something or someone

Language points

Nouns (an object, a person, or an animal) ■ Indefinite articles **un, uno, una, un'** ■ Plurals of nouns ■ **Chi è?** ■ **Cos'è? (Cosa è?)** ■ **questo, questa, questi, queste**

Introduction

Study these examples of things you might want to ask for in Italy:

Un cappuccino, per favore.	*A coffee, please.*
Una cioccolata, per piacere	*A hot chocolate, please*
... e una spremuta.	*... and a fresh fruit juice.*
Due paste e due cappuccini.	*Two cakes and two cappuccinos.*

You might want to know what something is:

Che cos'è?	*What is it?*
È un telefonino.	*It's a mobile phone.*

Or what several things are:

Che cosa sono questi?	*What are these?*
Sono biscotti per Carnevale.	*They're biscuits for Carnival time.*

Or who somebody is:

Chi è?	*Who is he?*
È un turista americano.	*He's an American tourist.*
Chi sono?	*Who are they?*
Sono turisti inglesi.	*They're English tourists.*

Focus on grammar

1 Nouns and indefinite articles un, una, *etc*

A noun is a person, an animal, an object, or an abstract thing. In Italian, objects, as well as people, are either masculine or feminine. There are several different ways of saying *a* or *an* (**un, uno, una, un'**); the forms depend on whether the noun is masculine or feminine, and whether it starts with a vowel or a consonant. It is normally helpful to look at the ending of the word:

a) Nouns that end in *-o*

Nouns that end in **-o** are usually masculine. The definite article is normally **un**; but if they start with **s** plus another consonant, **gn, ps, z** or (usually) **pn** or **x**, it is **uno**.

un cappuccino	*a cappuccino*
un espresso	*an espresso*
uno spuntino	*a snack*
uno zoo	*a zoo*
uno psicologo	*a psychologist*

Exceptions: a few nouns end in **-o** but are feminine, for example:

una mano	*a hand*

b) Nouns that end in *-a*

Nouns that end in **-a** are usually feminine. These have the indefinite article **una**, or **un'** if they start with a vowel (**a, e, i, o, u**):

una cioccolata	*a hot chocolate*
una pasta	*a cake*
una spremuta	*a fresh fruit juice*
un'aranciata	*an orangeade*

Exceptions: a few nouns end in **-a** but are masculine, for example:

un programma	*a programme*
un cinema	*a cinema*

In unit 1, you saw some words denoting professions that end in **-ista** for both sexes. Their articles are **un** or **uno** for men or **una** or **un'** for women:

un pianista **/ una** pianista	*a pianist*
un artista **/ un'**artista	*an artist*
uno specialista **/ una** specialista	*a specialist*

c) Nouns that end in -e

Some nouns that end in **-e** are masculine (these take **un** or **uno**) and some are feminine (these take **una** or **un'**).

un giornale	*a newspaper*	**una** lezione	*a lesson*
uno studente	*a student (male)*	**un'**automobile	*a car*

d) Foreign words

Words borrowed from other languages, particularly those without a final vowel, are usually masculine so they take **un** or **uno**:

un bar	*a café, bar*	**un** toast	*a toasted sandwich*
un sandwich	*a sandwich*	**un** weekend	*a weekend*
un club	*a club*	**un** whisky	*a whisky*

But not always:

una brioche   *a brioche*

For some further examples of nouns that do not fit the patterns shown above, refer to the Grammar Appendix (1) at the end of the book.

Summary

Here are examples of the various types of nouns set out in table form, with **un, una**, etc.:

un cappuccino	**una** cioccolata
un aperitivo	**un'**aranciata
uno spuntino	**una** spremuta
un giornale	**una** chiave
un bar	

e) Male and female

You may be surprised to learn that – grammatically speaking – Italian does not always have a male and a female of each animal species:

una giraffa (*giraffe*) is always female
un ippopotamo (*hippopotamus*) is always male

In order to provide the missing half, you have to say:

| una giraffa maschio | *a male giraffe* |
| un ippopotamo femmina | *a female hippopotamus* |

Some animals – as in English – have a different name for the male and the female of the species:

| un cane *(dog)* | una cagna *(bitch)* |
| un gallo *(cock)* | una gallina *(hen)* |

2 Nouns (plural forms)

a) Nouns that end in -o
Masculine nouns that end in **-o** end in **-i** in the plural:

| un cappuccino | due cappuccini | *(two cappuccinos)* |
| uno spuntino | due spuntini | *(two snacks)* |

So does this feminine noun:

| una mano | due mani | *(two hands)* |

This noun has an irregular plural:

| un uomo | due uomini | *(two men)* |

b) Nouns that end in -a

Feminine nouns ending in **-a** end in **-e** in the plural:

| una cioccolata | due cioccolate | *two chocolates* |
| una spremuta | due spremute | *two fresh fruit juices* |

Masculine nouns that end in **-a** end in **-i** in the plural:

| un programma | due programmi | *two programmes* |

For nouns describing people, such as **artista**, where both genders exist, masculine nouns in the plural end in **-i (artisti)**, while feminine nouns end in **-e (artiste)**, for example:

un artista	due artisti	*two artists* (male)
un'artista	due artiste	*two artists* (female)
uno stilista	due stilisti	*two designers* (male)
una stilista	due stiliste	*two stylists* (female)

c) Nouns that end in -e

Masculine nouns ending in **-e** end in **-i** when they are plural:

| un giornal**e** | due giornal**i** | *two newspapers* |
| uno student**e** | due student**i** | *two students* |

So do feminine nouns:

| una lezion**e** | due lezion**i** | *two lessons* |
| un'automobil**e** | due automobil**i** | *two cars* |

d) Words that don't change in the plural

Words borrowed from other languages:

un bar	due bar	*two bars*
un sandwich	due sandwich	*two sandwiches*
una brioche	due brioche	*two brioches*

Words ending in an accented vowel:

una citt**à**	due citt**à**	*two cities*
un caff**è**	due caff**è**	*two coffees*
un t**è**	due t**è**	*two teas*

For further examples of nouns that do not fit the patterns shown above, please refer to the Grammar Appendix (1).

Summary

Here are examples of the various types of nouns and their plural forms set out in table form:

un cappuccin**o**	due cappuccin**i**	una past**a**	due past**e**
uno spuntin**o**	due spuntin**i**	una spremut**a**	due spremut**e**
un amar**o**	due amar**i**	un'aranciat**a**	due aranciat**e**
un giornal**e**	due giornal**i**	una chiav**e**	due chiav**i**
un bar	due bar		

3 Chi è?

To ask who someone is **chi** (*who*) and **è** (*he/she/it is*) are used:

Chi è? *Who is it?*

And for more than one person **Chi sono?**

Chi sono?	*Who are they?*
È Giorgio.	*It's Giorgio.*
Sono Paolo e Giulia.	*They're Paolo and Giulia.*

4 Che cos'è?

To ask what something is, you say: **che** *(what)* and **cosa** *(thing)* and **è**. Before **è**, **cosa** is usually abbreviated:

Che cos'è *or*	*What is it?* (Lit: *what thing is it?*)
Cos'è?	
È un elenco telefonico.	*It's a telephone directory.*

For more than one thing, you say:

Che cosa sono? *or*	*What are they?*
Cosa sono?	
Sono biscotti per Carnevale.	*They're biscuits for Carnival.*

Language plus

Questo

To make it quite clear who or what you are referring to, you can point, and/or you can add **questo** to your question or your reply. **Questo** *(this* or *this thing* or *this person)*, indicates something or someone near you. It has different forms **(questo, questa, questi, queste)** according to whether the object or person referred to is singular or plural, masculine or feminine.

Pointing out an object

Masculine singular:

Questo è un aperitivo sardo.	*This is an aperitif from Sardinia.*
Cos'è **questo**?	*What's this?*
È un aperitivo sardo.	*It's an aperitif from Sardinia.*

Feminine singular:

Questa è una bibita analcolica.	*This is a non-alcoholic drink.*
Cos'è **questa**?	*What is this?*
È una bibita analcolica.	*It's a non-alcoholic drink.*

Masculine plural:

Questi sono gnocchi di patate.	*These are potato gnocchi.*
Cosa sono **questi**?	*What are these?*
Sono gnocchi di patate.	*They're potato gnocchi.*

Feminine plural:

Queste sono paste di mandorla.	*These are almond cakes.*
Cosa sono **queste**?	*What are these?*
Sono paste di mandorla.	*They're almond cakes.*

Note: Gnocchi are very small 'dumplings' made out of semolina or potato (**gnocchi di patate**), served with a sauce and usually eaten for the first course as a change from pasta. While **pasta** means pasta (**spaghetti**, **tagliatelle**, etc.) **una pasta** can also mean a small individual cake. (**Torta** or **dolce** are meant for sharing!).

Indicating or introducing a person

Chi è **questo**?	*Who is this?*
È Luigi.	*It's Luigi.*
Chi è **questa**?	*Who is this (woman)?*
Questa è una turista americana.	*This is an American tourist.*
Chi sono **questi**?	*Who are these (people)?*
Sono Henry e Henrietta.	*They're Henry and Henrietta.*
Chi sono **queste**?	*Who are these (women)?*
Queste sono turiste americane.	*These are American tourists.*

Questo or *questa*?

With people it's obvious when to use **questo** and **questa** but with objects it's not so easy. It's safest to assume it's masculine and use **questo** (**questi** if it's plural):

Chi è **questo**?	*Who is this (man)?*
È un professore.	*He's a teacher.*
Chi è **questa**?	*Who is this (woman)?*
È un'amica.	*She's a friend.*
Cos'è **questo/ questa**?	*What's this?*
È una spremuta d'arancia.	*It's a fresh orange juice.*

Questo can also be found used as an adjective. See unit 5.

Language in action

Exercise 1

Un, una, uno, un'

Fill in the gaps with the correct form of indefinite article. If you have not met the word before, this is a chance to look it up in your dictionary and find out what gender it is:

.... cornetto   .... caffè   .... spremuta
.... birra   .... cappuccino   .... aperitivo
.... brioche   .... aranciata   .... digestivo
.... toast   .... limonata
.... bicchiere di acqua minerale

Exercise 2

Now you decide you want two of everything you have just ordered.

e.g. Un cornetto?
    No, due cornetti.

Exercise 3

In a bar

You are now ready to order some items for your friends! Here are some words to help you:

    per favore, per piacere   *please*
    un cornetto   *Italian version of a croissant, plain, filled with jam or
                  pastry cream and generally eaten in mornings.
                  Nothing to do with ice-cream.*
    un cono   *ice-cream cone*
    un aperitivo   *aperitif (for before the meal)*
    un digestivo   *digestif (for after the meal)*

Order the items you see in the pictures below:

3 | ASKING ABOUT AVAILABILITY

Learn how to ...

■ Ask and say if something or someone exists ■ Say where something/someone is ■ Ask and say if something is available ■ Say how much there is

Language points

c'è, ci sono ■ ne ■ dei, delle, degli and del, della, etc. ■ alcuni, alcune ■ qualche ■ un po' di

Introduction

First, look at these examples:

C'è un telefono qui vicino? — *Is there a telephone near here?*
Sì, ce n'è uno al Bar Roma. — *Yes, there's one at the Roma bar.*

Ci sono tortellini oggi? — *Are there tortellini today?*
Sì. Ce ne sono. — *Yes. There are (some).*

Ci sono turisti a Lecce? — *Are there any tourists at Lecce?*
Sì, ce ne sono alcuni. — *Yes, there are a few.*

Ci sono anche degli stranieri? — *Are there foreigners too?*
Ci sono dei tedeschi e qualche inglese. — *There are Germans, and a few English.*

Focus on grammar

1 C'è, ci sono

In unit 1 you learned **essere** *(to be)*. If you put it together with **ci** *(there)* you get **c'è** *(there is)* which is short for **ci è,** and the plural **ci sono** *(there are)*:

C'è una cabina telefonica all'angolo.	*There is a telephone box at the corner.*
Ci sono studenti italiani.	*There are Italian students.*

Make it sound like a question by raising your voice at the end, as you learnt in unit 1:

C'è ...? *Is there ...?*	**Ci sono ...?** *Are there ...?*
C'è una toilette?	*Is there a toilet?*
Sì, c'è una toilette.	*Yes, there's a toilet.*
C'è un medico?	*Is there a doctor?*
Sì, c'è un medico.	*Yes, there's a doctor.*
Ci sono pesche oggi?	*Are there peaches today?*
Sì, oggi ci sono pesche.	*Yes, today there are peaches.*

2 Ne

When answering a question (**C'è un telefono?**), instead of repeating the object (**Sì, c'è un telefono**) you can use **ne** *(of it, of them)* and either **uno/una** *(one)* or other number or a quantity. When **ci** and **ne** are combined, **ci** becomes **ce** as in **ce n'è, ce ne sono** *there is (one, some), there are (some)*:

C'è un telefono?	*Is there a telephone?*
Sì, **ce n'è** uno.	*Yes, there is one (of them).*
Ci sono delle guide?	*Are there any guides?*
Sì, **ce ne sono** due.	*Yes, there are two (of them).*
Ci sono dei fichi freschi oggi?	*Are there any fresh figs today?*
Sì, **ce ne sono** tanti.	*Yes, there are lots (of them).*

One will be either **uno** or **una** depending on whether the object or person is masculine or feminine, for example:

C'è un medico?	*Is there a doctor?*
Sì, ce n'è **uno**.	*Yes, there is one (of them).*
C'è una toilette?	*Is there a toilet?*
Sì, ce n'è **una**.	*Yes, there is one.*

To say that there aren't any:

C'è un telefono?	*Is there are a telephone?*
No. **Non c'è**.	*No. There isn't one.*
Ci sono studenti qui?	*Are there any students here?*
No. **Non ce ne sono**.	*No. There aren't any.*

Generally, **ne** is used in the singular only when there is a number or other indication of quantity, as shown in these examples:

C'è un bicchiere?	*Is there a glass?*
Sì, **c'è**.	*Yes, there is.*
Sì, **ce n'è uno**.	*Yes, there is one.*

3 Expressing 'some'

Some is expressed in Italian in several different words and phrases. Some expressions can only be used when there is more than one thing or person involved. Others can only be used after a negative, translating the English *any*.

4 Dei, delle *and* del, della, *etc*

The forms of **dei, delle** (*some, any*) vary to match the noun they go with, i.e. masculine or feminine (see unit 2). For plural masculine nouns, use **dei**; but use **degli** if the noun starts with a vowel, or **s** plus another consonant, or **gn, pn, ps, x** or **z**. For feminine nouns the correct form is **delle**. Here are some examples:

Ci sono **dei** biscotti al cioccolato.	*There are some chocolate biscuits.*
Ci sono **delle** paste di mandorla.	*There are some almond cakes.*
Ci sono **degli** zucchini al burro.	*There are courgettes done in butter.*
Ci sono **degli** alberghi in centro.	*There are some hotels in the centre.*
Ci sono **delle** melanzane?	*Are there any aubergines?*
Sì, ci sono **delle** melanzane bellissime oggi.	*Yes, there are some beautiful aubergines today.*

The singular forms **del, della**, etc. can also be used to express *some*. Taking the endings of the definite articles (**il, lo**, etc.), you use **del** for a masculine noun, **della** for a feminine noun, **dello** before a masculine noun beginning with **s** plus another consonant, or **gn, ps, ps, x** or **z,** and **dell'** for a noun beginning with a vowel:

Vorrei **del** vino.	*I'd like some wine.*
Prendo **dello** zucchero.	*I'll take some sugar.*
C'è **della** marmellata di fragola.	*There is some strawberry jam.*
Vorrei **dell'**aranciata.	*I'd like some orangeade.*
Vuole **dell'**Amaretto di Saronno?	*Would you like some Amaretto di Saronno?*

5 Alcuni, alcune

Another way of expressing *some* (plural nouns only) is to use **alcuni** (for masculine nouns) or **alcune** (for feminine nouns). **Alcun** is never used in the singular except with a negative meaning (see Grammar Appendix, 5.1). **Alcuni** suggests the idea of *a few,* rather than *several,* and can be used as an adjective (describing a noun) or as a pronoun (on its own) meaning *a few things, a few people*:

Ci sono **alcuni** problemi.	*There are a few problems.*
Ci sono **alcune** cose da fare prima di partire.	*There are a few things to do before leaving.*

The construction **ce ne sono** can also be used with **alcuni**; in this case **alcuni** stands on its own, without a noun:

Ci sono dei giornali italiani?	*Are there any Italian newspapers?*
Ce ne sono **alcuni**.	*There are a few (of them).*

6 Qualche

Qualche is similar in meaning to **alcuni**; it means *a few, some* and is always used in the singular form but with plural meaning. It can only be used with nouns that can be counted separately and individually and *not* with 'uncountable' nouns like *sugar:*

C'è **qualche programma** interessante stasera?	*Are there any interesting programmes on TV tonight*?
C'è **qualche amico** di Marco a casa.	*There are a few friends of Marco's at home.*

7 Un po' di

The phrase **un po' di** (short for **un poco di**, *a little*), can be used both for singular 'uncountable' nouns such as *sugar, wine, bread, butter* or for plural 'countable' wines such as *biscuits, cakes, breadsticks*:

| **un po' di** vino | *a little wine* | **un po' di** grissini | *a few breadsticks* |
| **un po' di** caffè | *a little coffee* | **un po' di** paste | *a few cakes* |

Language plus

1 Non...nessun(o)

To emphasise that there isn't or there aren't any, use **non** and the negative form **nessuno** *(no, not any)* which varies in the same way as **un, uno, una, un'**:

Non c'è **nessuna** guida.	*There is no guide.*
Non c'è **nessun'**automobile disponibile.	*There are no cars available.* (Lit: *there is no car.*)
Non c'è **nessun** posto.	*There is no room.*
Non c'è **nessuno** scrittore interessante.	*There are no interesting writers.*

In unit 19 you can find out what happens when you 'qualify' statements such as the above with an additional specification, for example:

| **Non** c'è **nessuno** scrittore moderno **che mi piaccia.** | *There are no modern writers that I like.* |

2 Qualcosa, qualcuno, nessuno, niente

While **qualche** and **nessun** are adjectives and are used with a noun, the pronouns **qualcosa** (*something, anything*), **qualcuno** (*someone, anyone*) and **nessuno** (*nobody*) can be used on their own, as can **niente**:

C'è **qualcosa** da mangiare?	*Is there anything to eat?*
C'è **qualcuno**?	*Is anyone there?*
Non c'è **nessuno**.	*There's no-one there.*
È venuto **qualcuno**.	*Someone came.*
Non c'è **niente** da mangiare.	*There is nothing to eat.*

Language in action

Exercise 1

Silvia's party

What is there to eat and drink at Silvia's drinks party? Below is a list. Add the correct form of **del, alcuni, qualche** or **un po' di** to each item. Practise using as many '*some*' words as possible.

e.g. panini
  dei panini / alcuni panini / qualche panino / un po' di panini

salatini	patatine	pastine	stuzzicchini	grissini
pizzette	spuntini	bibite	aperitivi	coca cola
aranciata	vino	birra	alcolici	analcolici
uova sode	acqua	liquori	gelato	dolce

Exercise 2

Use the pictures to say how much there is of each item:

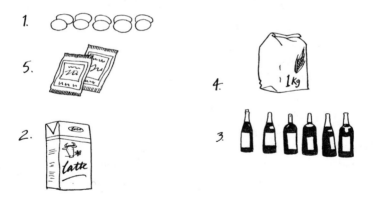

e.g. Quanto parmigiano c'è?   **Ce n'è un chilo.**

1 Quante uova ci sono?   4 Quanta farina c'è?
2 Quanto latte c'è?   5 Quanto lievito c'è?
3 Quanto vino c'è?

For more on **quanto**, see unit 5.

4 | TALKING ABOUT LOCATION

Learn how to ...

■ Ask where something or someone is ■ Say where something or someone is

Language points

■ **il, la, lo,** etc. (definite article) ■ Plurals of nouns ■ **dov'è, dove sono?** ■ **in, a, da, su** and all the combined forms **nel, al, dal, sul** ■ Phrases indicating location **in centro, in primo piano,** etc. ■ **Ecco** and **mi, ti, lo, la** (direct object pronouns)

Introduction

Study these examples of questions and answers about location:

Dov'è il Bar Roma?	*Where is Bar Roma?*
È in Via dei Sette Santi.	*It's in Via dei Sette Santi.*
Dove sono gli scavi?	*Where are the excavations?*
Sono in fondo a questa strada.	*They're at the bottom of this road.*
Dov'è il telefono?	*Where is the phone?*
È nell'angolo.	*It's in the corner.*
Dove sono gli elenchi telefonici?	*Where are the telephone directories?*
Sono dietro il banco.	*They're behind the counter.*
Peter e Mara abitano a Londra, in Inghilterra.	*Peter and Mara live in London, England.*

Focus on grammar

1 il, lo, la, *etc*

In unit 2 you saw that **un** *(a,an)* varies according to the gender of the noun (person or thing). The same thing happens with **il, lo, la** *(the)*, the definite article.

Look at these examples:

Singular	
Dov'è **il** bar?	*Where is the café?*
Dov'è **la** stazione?	*Where is the station?*
Dov'è **l'**automobile?	*Where is the car?*
Dov'è **lo** stadio?	*Where is the stadium?*
Dov'è **l'**albergo?	*Where is the hotel?*
Plural	
Dove sono **i** bambini?	*Where are the children?*
Dove sono **le** ragazze?	*Where are the girls?*
Dove sono **gli** studenti?	*Where are the students?*
Dove sono **gli** alberghi?	*Where are the hotels?*

a) Nouns ending in *-o*

Masculine nouns ending in **-o** take the article **il**; they take **lo** if they start with **s** plus another consonant, or with **gn, pn, ps, x** or **z**; they take **l'** if they start with a vowel.

In the plural, masculine nouns take the article **i**; but take **gli** if they begin with **s** plus a consonant, or **gn, pn, ps, x, z,** or if they start with a vowel.

Singular		**Plural**	
il ragazzo	*the boy*	**i** ragazzi	*the boys*
lo stadio	*the stadium*	**gli st**adi	*the stadiums*
l'albergo	*the hotel*	**gli a**lberghi	*the hotels*

There are a few feminine nouns ending in **-o** and these take the article **la**. The plural of such nouns is also irregular:

Singular		Plural	
la mano	*the hand*	**le** mani	*the hands*
la radio	*the radio*	**le** radio	*the radios*

b) Nouns ending in -*a*

Most nouns ending in **-a** are feminine and take **la**; they take **l'** if they start with a vowel. With the plural form, the article used is **le**:

Singular		Plural	
la ragazza	*the girl*	**le** ragazze	*the girls*
la studentessa	*the student* (fem)	**le** studentesse	*the students*
l'arancia	*the orangeade*	**le** aranciate	*the orangeades*

Some nouns ending in **-a** are masculine and take **il** or **lo**. The plural is regular, taking the article **i**:

> **il** programma *the programme*   **i** programmi *the programmes*

There are several words ending in **-ista** which denote professions *(see unit 2)* and which can be either masculine (taking **il, lo, l'**) or feminine (taking **la, l'**).

In the plural, the masculine nouns end in **-i**, and take the article **i** or **gli**, while the feminine nouns end in **-e** and take the article **le**:

Singular		Plural
il pianista	*(the pianist, male)*	**i** pianisti
la pianista	*(the pianist, female)*	**le** pianiste
lo specialista	*(the specialist, male)*	**gli** specialisti
la specialista	*(the specialist, female)*	**le** specialiste
l'artista	*(the artist, male/female)*	**gli** artisti *or* **le** artiste

c) Nouns ending in -*e*

Some nouns ending in **-e** are masculine, taking **il**; but **lo** before **s** plus another consonant and before **gn, pn, ps, x** and **z**; they take **l'** before a vowel. Some are feminine, taking **la**, or **l'** before a vowel. The plural forms end in **-i** and take the article **i** or **gli** for the masculine nouns, and **le** for feminine nouns:

Singular		**Plural**	
il giornale	*the newspaper*	**i** giornali	*the newspapers*
lo studente	*the student*	**gli** studenti	*the students*
la lezione	*the lesson*	**le** lezioni	*the lessons*
l'automobile	*the car*	**le** automobili	*the cars*

2 Dov'è ...?, dove sono ...?

The word **dove** means *where*: it combines with **è** when you want to ask where something is, and **sono** to ask where several things are:

Dov'è il cameriere?	*Where is the waiter?*
Dove sono i biscotti?	*Where are the biscuits?*
Dove sono gli studenti?	*Where are the students?*
Dov'è l'Ufficio Cambio?	*Where is the Bureau de Change?*

3 Location a, in, da, *etc*

To say where something is, you often use a preposition, such as *in, at, to,* for example:

in centro	*in the centre*
a Roma	*in Rome*
in Italia	*in Italy*

Whether saying *to* or *in* a place, Italians use **a** with a town or city, and **in** with a country.

a Londra	*in London/to London*
in Inghilterra	*in England/to England*

Da has no exact equivalent in English; it means *at the house of, at the shop/restaurant of*:

da Carmelo	*at Carmelo's (house, shop, restaurant)*
da Maria	*at Maria's (house, shop or restaurant)*

It is often used as a name for a restaurant:

| **da** Lorenzo | *Lorenzo's* |

4 *Prepositions combined with articles* **al, nel, dal, sul**

a + il, etc.

al ristorante	*at/to the restaurant*
allo stadio	*at/to the stadium*
all'albergo	*at/to the hotel*
all'accademia	*at/to the academy*
alla spiaggia	*at/to the beach*
ai laghi	*at/to the lakes*
agli alberghi	*at/to the hotels*
agli sportelli	*at/to the ticket windows*
***alle stelle!**	*at/to the stars!*

I prezzi sono alle stelle *means 'the prices are very expensive'.*

in + il, etc.

nel ristorante	*in the restaurant*
nello specchio	*in the mirror*
nell'ufficio	*in the office*
nell'acqua	*in the water*
nella camera	*in the bedroom*
nei giardini	*in the gardens*
negli alberi	*in the trees*
negli scavi	*in the excavations*
nelle camere	*in the bedrooms*

dal medico	*at the doctor's*
dallo psichiatra	*at the psychiatrist's*
dall'amico	*at the* (male) *friend's* (house)
dall'amica	*at the* (female) *friend's* (house)
dalla zia	*at the aunt's house*
dai ragazzi	*at the boys' house*
dagli americani	*at the Americans' house*
dagli studenti	*at the students' house*
dalle ragazze	*at the girls' house*

Lastly, **su** *(on)* can be combined with the definite article **il**, etc. to create compound forms:

sul banco	*on the counter*
sullo sgabello	*on the stool*
sull'albero	*on the tree*
sull'isola	*on the island*
sulla sabbia	*on the sand*
sui gradini	*on the steps*
sugli alberi	*on the trees*
sugli scalini	*on the steps*
sulle scale	*on the stairs*

In frequently used phrases, Italian tends to miss out the article and just use the simple form **in, a**, etc.

in centro	*in the centre*
in giardino	*in the garden*
a casa	*at home*
a scuola	*at school*

5 Adverbs and prepositions expressing location

qui	*here*	in cima a	*at the top of*
lì	*there*	vicino	*near*
in alto	*high up, up there*	lontano	*far*
in basso	*down there, at the bottom*	dietro	*behind*
		davanti	*in front of*
giù	*down (there)*	dentro	*inside*
in vetrina	*in the (shop) window*	fuori	*outside*
in mezzo	*in the middle*	accanto	*next to*
a sinistra	*on the left*	di fronte a	*oposite*
a destra	*on the right*	sopra	*above*
in fondo	*in the background*	sotto	*under*
in primo piano	*in the foreground*	verso	*toward*

Some prepositions expressing place are always combined with another preposition:

accanto **al** banco, vicino **all'**albergo, lontano **dal** centro, davanti **a** noi

while others need one only before a pronoun:

dentro il cinema	*but*	dentro **di** me
verso la stazione	*but*	verso **di** noi
dietro il castello	*but*	dietro **a** lui

Language plus

1 Ecco!

An easy way to reply to *where* questions is to use the word **ecco** which means *Here is, here are* or *There is, there are:*

Dov'è il telefono?	*Where is the telephone?*
Ecco il telefono!	*There's the telephone.*
Dove sono gli elenchi telefonici?	*Where are the telephone directories?*
Ecco gli elenchi!	*Here are the directories!*

Ecco can also stand on its own, and can be used when someone hands you something (English *There you are!*) or has just completed something, in which case **ecco** is often combined with the word **fatto** (*done*):

Ecco fatto!	*That's that!*

2 Ecco *and* mi, ti, lo, la, *etc*

Ecco can also be combined with **mi, ti, lo, la,** etc. to form a phrase meaning *Here I am* or *Here it is.* **Mi, ti, lo, la,** etc. are pronouns; they are used in place of a noun, whether person or inanimate object. They are usually found linked directly to a verb (see unit 14) which is why they are known as direct object pronouns. Their form will depend on whether the person or object they are replacing is masculine or feminine, singular or plural. Here are some examples:

Dove sei, Susy?	*Where are you, Susy?*
Ecco**mi**!	*Here I am!*
Dov'è il barista?	*Where is the barman?*
Ecco**lo**!	*Here he is! / There he is!*

Dov'è la stazione?	*Where is the station?*
Ecco**la**!	*There it is!*
Dove sono i bambini?	*Where are the children?*
Ecco**ci**!	*Here we are!*
Dove sono le pile?	*Where are the batteries?*
Ecco**le**!	*Here they are!*

Finally, here is a full picture of all the direct object pronouns:

Singular		**Plural**	
mi	*me*	ci	*us*
ti	*you* (informal)	vi	*you* (plural)
lo	*it, him*	li	*them*
la	*it, her*	le	*them*
La	*you* (formal)		

Language in action

Exercise 1

Your friend is coming to stay in your house while you are away. Tell her where everything is. You will need to fill in the gaps either with the plain preposition **in** or a combination of the definite article and appropriate preposition **a, in, su (al, nel, sul,** etc):

1 Il latte è .... frigorifero.
2 Le tazzine sono .... armadietto .... cucina.
3 L'impianto stereo è .... soggiorno.
4 Il gatto è .... giardino.
5 La lavatrice è .... bagno.
6 Le lenzuola sono .... cassettone.
7 Il telecomando è vicino .... poltrona.
8 I libri italiani sono .... camera degli ospiti.
9 I dizionari sono .... scaffale .... studio.
10 Le chiavi sono .... cassetto della credenza.

Exercise 2

Dialogo (Turista/residente)

Using the map for information, tell a tourist where he can find certain places:

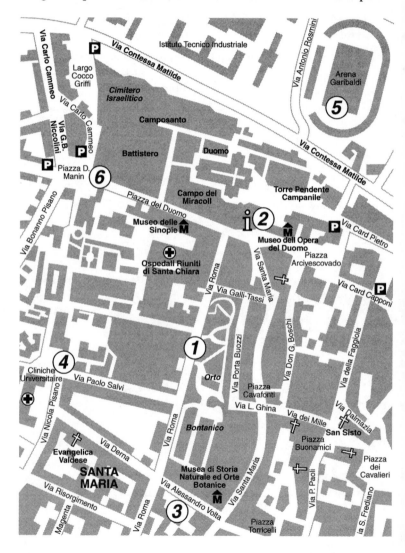

e.g. Scusi, dov'è l'albergo Rondinella**?**

L'albergo Rondinella? È in Piazza Treviso, vicino alla stazione.

1 Dove sono i grandi magazzini?
   Sono in .... vicino a ....

2 Dov'è l'Ente Provinciale di Turismo?
   È in .... vicino a ....

3 Dove sono le cabine telefoniche?
   Sono in .... vicino a ....

4 Dov'è la biblioteca?
   È in .... vicino a ....

5 Dov'è la Pensione Ginestra?
   È in .... vicino a ....

6 Dov'è il parcheggio?
   È in .... vicino a ....

5 | STATING CHOICE AND PREFERENCE

Learn how to ...

■ Ask the cost of a thing or things ■ Express a preference ■ Specify which item you want ■ Use numbers ■ Ask how much or how many

Language points

■ **questo/quello** ■ **quanto?** ■ Verbs ending in **-are**, e.g. **costare**
■ Verbs ending in **-ere**, e.g. **prendere** ■ Numbers ■ **quale?**

Introduction

Look at these examples:

Quanto costa questo?	*How much does this cost?*
Quanto costano questi sandali?	*How much do these sandals cost?*
Questi costano centocinquantamila lire.	*These cost L150.000 lire.*
Prendiamo queste due cartoline.	*We'll take these two postcards.*
Quanto costa quello?	*How much does that cost?*
Quanto costano quelle scarpe?	*How much do those shoes cost?*
Prendo quel borsellino in vetrina.	*I'll take that purse in the window.*
Prendo quelli.	*I'll take those ones.*

Focus on grammar

1 Questo *or* quello

Demonstrative adjectives and pronouns (English *this, that)* are used to indicate or 'demonstrate' the object or person referred to. Italian uses **questo** (*this*) and **quello** (*that*).

2 Questo

Questo is used to indicate something or someone near the speaker. When **questo** is used as an adjective, describing a person or thing, it changes its ending according to whether the person or thing is singular or plural, masculine or feminine. There are four possible forms:

Singular	
Questo museo è chiuso.	**Questa** casa è sporca.
This museum is shut.	*This house is dirty.*
Plural	
Questi biglietti sono cari.	**Queste** camere sono piccole.
These tickets are dear.	*These rooms are small.*

Questo can also be used as a pronoun, i.e. on its own in place of a noun, meaning *this (one), these (ones)* (see unit 2).

> **Questo** è difficile. *This is difficult.*

Questo used on its own still has to vary its ending according to the gender and number of the thing/person it is referring to (**questo, questa, questi, queste**), but if you don't know what it is called in Italian, far less the gender, just point and use **questo** (or **questi** if it's plural)!

Questi sono belli.	*These are beautiful.*
*Quale gonna vuole misurare? **Questa**.	*Which skirt do you want to try on?* *This one.*
Quali scarpe vuole provare? **Queste**.	*Which shoes do you want to try on?* *These ones.*

Quale means *which*. The plural form is **quali**. If you want to know more, read the Language plus section.

3 Quello

Use **quello** *(that)* to indicate something which is not near the speaker. Its forms vary in exactly the same way as the article **il** *(the)*, according to whether the noun is masculine, feminine, singular or plural and according to the initial letter. Here are the forms of **quello** when used as an adjective:

Singular

Quel ristorante è sporco.	*That restaurant is dirty.*
Quell'albergo è di lusso.	*That hotel is a luxury one.*
Quello scontrino è sbagliato.	*That receipt is wrong.*
Quella pensione costa poco.	*That pension is cheap.*
Quell'agenzia è chiusa.	*That agency is closed.*

Plural

Quei sandali sono di plastica.	*Those sandals are plastic.*
Quegli stivali sono brutti.	*Those boots are ugly.*
Quegli alberghi sono economici.	*Those hotels are cheap.*
Quelle scarpe sono di pelle.	*Those shoes are leather.*

Like **questo, quello** can also be used on its own. Use **quello** (singular) or **quelli** (plural) if you are uncertain of the gender:

Quello è incredibile.	*That (person or thing) is unbelievable.*
Quelli sono antipatici.	*Those (people) are unpleasant.*
Quella è carina.	*That (girl) is pretty.*
Quelle sono simpatiche.	*Those (girls) are nice.*

4 Quanto

Quanto can be used as an adjective, along with a person/object, meaning *how much* or *how many*. **Quanto** varies according to whether the noun is masculine, feminine, singular, or plural. Or it can be used on its own, meaning *how much,* in which case it doesn't change:

Quanto zucchero prendi?	*How much sugar do you take?*
Quanta pasta mangi?	*How much pasta do you eat?*
Quanti panini prendi?	*How many sandwiches are you having?*
Quante sigarette fumi al giorno?	*How many cigarettes do you smoke a day?*
Quanto costa?	*How much does it cost?*
Quanto ti fermi?	*How long are you staying? (Lit: How much time are you stopping?)*

5 -are and -ere verbs

The pronouns **io, tu, lui**, etc. (see unit 1) are not needed with the verb in Italian because the endings show who or what is doing the action, in other words, who or what is the subject of the sentence. The pronoun can, however, be used for emphasis as shown below in brackets.

Most Italian verbs follow one of three main patterns. They end in **-are, -ere** or **-ire**.

Verbs ending in -are

Verbs are usually listed in a dictionary in the infinitive form. An example is **parlare** *(to talk)*:

parlare					
(io)	parl**o**	*I speak*	(noi)	parl**iamo**	*we speak*
(tu)	parl**i**	*you speak*	(voi)	parl**ate**	*you speak*
(lui)	parl**a**	*he speaks*	(loro)	parl**ano**	*they speak*
(lei)	parl**a**	*she speaks*			
(Lei)	parl**a**	*you speak* (formal)			

Verbs ending in -ere

An example of this pattern is **prendere** (to take, to have e.g. *something to eat or drink*):

prendere					
(io)	prend**o**	*I take*	(noi)	prend**iamo**	*we speak*
(tu)	prend**i**	*you take*	(voi)	prend**ete**	*you speak*
(lui)	prend**e**	*he takes*	(loro)	prend**ono**	*they speak*
(lei)	prend**e**	*she takes*			
(Lei)	prend**e**	*you take* (formal)			

Verbs ending in -ire

There is a third group of verbs ending in **-ire** (see unit 6). They do not vary much from **-ere** verbs.

Irregular verbs

Unfortunately some verbs don't follow a pattern; these are called 'irregular'. There is a list of the most common irregular verbs at the end of the book.

6 Numbers

1 to 20

0	zero	6	sei	12	dodici	18	diciotto
1	uno	7	sette	13	tredici	19	diciannove
2	due	8	otto	14	quattordici	20	venti
3	tre	9	nove	15	quindici		
4	quattro	10	dieci	16	sedici		
5	cinque	11	undici	17	diciassette		

21 to 30

21	ventuno	26	ventisei
22	ventidue	27	ventisette
23	ventitré	28	ventotto
24	ventiquattro	29	ventinove
25	venticinque	30	trenta

31 to 40 and up ...

31	trentuno	60	sessanta
32	trentadue	70	settanta
33	trentatré	80	ottanta
38	trentotto	90	novanta
40	quaranta	100	cento
50	cinquanta		

hundreds ...

101	centouno
102	centodue
140	centoquaranta
142	centoquarantadue
200	duecento
etc	

thousands ...

1000	mille
1001	mille (e) uno
1500	millecinquecento
1550	millecinquecentocinquanta
1555	millecinquecentocinquantacinque
2000	duemila
10.000	diecimila

millions ...

1.000.000	un milione
2.000.000	due milioni
1.500.255	un milionecinquecentomiladuecentocinquantacinque

billions ...

1.000.000.000	un miliardo

Notes:

- In **ventuno, ventotto** the **i** is dropped from **venti.**

- **Tre** does not have an accent on the last letter but **ventitré** does, as do all the compounds including **tre** from **ventitré** upwards.

- In **trentuno, trentotto** the **a** has been dropped from **trenta**; likewise all the other numbers ending in **-a** from 30 upwards.

- **cento** occasionally loses its final **o** as in **centottanta** (**cento ottanta**); **centotto** (**cento otto**).

- The plural of **mille** is **mila.**

- In English you say *one* hundred, *one* thousand; in Italian you omit the *one*: **cento** and **mille,** but note: **un** milione **di** abitanti *(one million inhabitants)* (the **di** is omitted when other numbers follow).

- Several digit numbers are generally written as one word, e.g.

    142   centoquarantadue

Ordinal numbers and fractions

The ordinal numbers *(first, second*, etc.) in Italian usually end in **-esimo**, e.g. **quindicesimo, ventesimo, centesimo**. But the first ten are as follows: **primo, secondo, terzo, quarto, quinto, sesto, settimo, ottavo, nono, decimo**. These can be abbreviated to 10°, 20°, etc.

These forms are also used to express fractions: **una decima parte** (*a tenth*); **un quarto** (*a quarter*); **due terzi** (*two-thirds*).

Language plus

1 Quale

Quale is an adjective meaning *which*. It has a singular form, **quale** and a plural form, **quali.**

Quale gelato vuoi?   *Which ice-cream do you want?*
Quali biscotti prendiamo?   *Which biscuits shall we get?*

It can also be used to translate English *what* in certain cases (see unit 10).

Language in action

Exercise 1

Quale preferisci?

You have a choice of items. Choosing one of the words supplied, specify which item you prefer or want to buy, making the adjective agree where necessary. (See unit 14 for **preferire**.)

e.g. Quale tavolo preferisci?   *(antico, moderno)*
  Preferisco quello moderno.

1 Quale casa preferisci?   *(in campagna, in città)*
2 Quale giacca prendi?   *(economico, caro)*
3 Quali sandali metti?   *(sportivo, elegante)*
4 Quali scarpe compri?   *(con tacco alto, senza tacco)*
5 Quali francobolli metti?   *(da L650, da L850)*
6 Quale panino prendi?   *(con prosciutto, con formaggio)*
7 Quali biscotti mangi?   *(con nocciola, con cioccolato)*
8 Quale vino bevi?   *(rosso, bianco)*
9 Quale giornale leggi?   *(inglese, italiano)*
10. Quali film guardi?   *(comico, romantico)*

Exercise 2

Opposites

Everything has an opposite. Use **questo** and **quello** to contrast the two items.

e.g. Queste scarpe sono comode. **Quelle** scarpe sono **strette**.

1 Quest'aranciata è fresca. .... aranciata è ....
2 Questo palazzo è vicino. .... palazzo è ....
3 Questi studenti sono in gamba. .... studenti sono ....
4 Questo albergo è di lusso. .... albergo è ....
5 Questi giornalisti sono onesti. .... giornalisti sono ....
6 Questa bottiglia è piena. .... bottiglia è ....
7 Questo film è interessante. .... film è ....
8 Questo museo è chiuso. .... museo è ....
9 Questo straniero è simpatico. .... straniero è ....
10 Questo specialista è vecchio. .... specialista è ....

6 TALKING ABOUT THE PRESENT

Learn how to ...

■ Ask or talk about the present ■ Ask or talk about where someone lives or works ■ Ask or talk about when someone does something

Language points

■ Verbs ending in **-ire** ■ **abitare, lavorare, studiare** ■ Question words **dove?, a che ora?, come?** ■ **stare** and gerund **-ando, endo** (immediate present)

Introduction

Study these examples of how to ask and answer questions about one's life and work:

Dove abiti, Lucia?
Abito in centro.

Where do you live, Lucia?
I live in the centre.

Lavori in città, Marco?
Sì, lavoro in banca.

Do you work in town, Marco?
Yes, I work in a bank.

A che ora cominci a lavorare?
Comincio alle otto.

What time do you start work?
I start work at 8 a.m.

A che ora finisci?
Finisco alle sette.

What time do you finish?
I finish at 7p.m.

Come vai a lavoro?
Prendo l'autobus.

How do you get to work?
I take the bus.

Com'è il tuo lavoro?
È interessante?

What is your work like?
Is it interesting?

Com'è Milano?

What is Milan like?

And how to talk about what you are doing right now ...

| Sto mangiando! | *I'm eating!* |
| Sto leggendo un libro. | *I'm reading a book.* |

Focus on grammar

1 -ire verbs

In unit 5 the verbs ending in **-are** and **-ere** were explained. Here we meet a new type of verb, ending in **-ire**:

---

finire *(to finish)*

(io)	fini**sco**	*I finish*	(noi)	fin**iamo**	*we finish*
(tu)	fini**sci**	*you finish*	(voi)	fin**ite**	*you finish*
(lui)	fini**sce**	*he finishes*	(loro)	fin**iscono**	*they finish*
(lei)	fini**sce**	*she finishes*			
(Lei)	fini**sce**	*you finish* (formal)			

Another verb which has this form is **preferire** *(to prefer)*.

There is another type of verb ending in **-ire**, which is much simpler:

---

dormire *(to sleep)*

(io)	dorm**o**	*I sleep*	(noi)	dorm**iamo**	*we sleep*
(tu)	dorm**i**	*you sleep*	(voi)	dorm**ite**	*you sleep*
(lui)	dorm**e**	*he sleeps*	(loro)	dorm**ono**	*they sleep*
(lei)	dorm**e**	*she sleeps*			
(Lei)	dorm**e**	*you sleep* (formal)			

Note the similarities in the different groups of verb: the *I, you, we* parts have the same ending:

I eat etc.	mang**io** / prend**o** / dorm**o** / fin**isco**
You eat, etc.	mang**i** / prend**i** / dorm**i** / fin**isci**
We eat, etc.	mang**iamo** / prend**iamo** / dorm**iamo** / fin**iamo**

2 Dove

Dove means *where* (see unit 4). You can use **dove** to ask where someone works or lives:

| **Dove** lavora Lei? | *Where do you work?* |
| **Dove** abitano i Rossi? | *Where do the Rossi family live?* |

Dove is abbreviated before **è** *(it is, is)*:

| **Dov'è** il bar? | *Where is the bar?* |
| Dove sono i bambini? | *Where are the children?* |

Although not strictly necessary, the pronoun **Lei** is often used when asking a question in the formal form, to make the question sound less abrupt:

| Dove abita **Lei?** | *Where do you work?* |

3 A che ora?

A che ora means literally *at what hour?*

A che ora comincia a lavorare?	*What time do you start work?* (using formal form)
A che ora chiude il negozio?	*What time does the shop close?*
A che ora parte il treno?	*What time does the train leave?*

4 Come?

Come used in a question means *how*:

Come arrivi al lavoro?	*How do you get to work?*
Come arrivi in centro?	*How do you get to the centre?*
Come comincia il film?	*How does the film begin?*
Come finisce la storia?	*How does the story end?*

Come is generally abbreviated before **è** to **com'è**. For further uses of **come**, see Grammar Appendix (10.11) at the end of the book.

5 Stare *(to be)* and gerund *(-ing form)*

Occasionally you need something more immediate than the simple present tense can convey to express something you are doing right now. For this, use the verb **stare** along with a part of the verb called the gerund, e.g. **mangiando, leggendo, partendo** (the Italian equivalent of the *-ing* ending) for example:

| I ragazzi **stanno leggendo**. | *The boys are reading.* |

The verb **stare** means *to be,* but cannot always replace **essere**; it is used only in the following contexts:

- in expressions such as **Come stai?** (*How are you?*)
- with the gerund **Sto mangiando, sto leggendo**, etc.
- to express geographical location as in **Dove sta la casa?** *(Where is the house?)*

a) *Stare*

The verb **stare** is irregular. Here is its present tense:

stare					
(io)	**sto**	*I am*	(noi)	**stiamo**	*we are*
(tu)	**stai**	*you are*	(voi)	**state**	*you are*
(lui)	**sta**	*he is*	(loro)	**stanno**	*they are*
(lei)	**sta**	*she is*			
(Lei)	**sta**	*you are* (formal)			

b) *Gerund*

The gerund is formed by taking the infinitive of the verb (for example **parlare**), removing **-are** and adding the ending **-ando**. Similarly, for **-ere** verbs, remove **-ere** and add **-endo**;   for **-ire** verbs remove **-ire** and add **-endo**:

parl**are**	*to speak*	parl**ando**	*speaking*
legg**ere**	*to read*	legg**endo**	*reading*
part**ire**	*to leave*	part**endo**	*leaving*

A few verbs (such as those with a shortened infinitive) have irregular gerund forms:

fare	*to do*	f**acendo**	*doing*
bere	*to drink*	b**evendo**	*drinking*

c) *Stare* and the gerund

Cosa **stai facendo**?	*What are you doing (right now)?*
Sto mettendo in ordine.	*I'm tidying up.*
Sto mangiando.	*I'm eating.*
Sto scrivendo una cartolina.	*I'm writing a postcard.*

Stare + gerund can not be used to talk about anything in the future, even if it's only tonight. For this you must use the plain present or the future.

Cosa fai stasera?	*What are you doing tonight?*

Language plus

1 Expressions of time

oggi	*today*
ieri	*yesterday*
domani	*tomorrow*

Oggi ti amo più di **ieri**, ma meno di **domani**.	*Today I love you more than yesterday, but less than tomorrow.*

stasera	*this evening*
stamattina	*this morning*
stanotte	*this night (last night)*
ieri sera	*yesterday evening*
ieri pomeriggio	*yesterday afternoon*
ieri notte	*last night*
domani mattina	*tomorrow morning*
domani pomeriggio	*tomorrow afternoon*
domani sera	*tomorrow evening*

2 Double adjectives

stanco morto	*dead tired*
ubriaco fradicio	*dead drunk* (Lit: *soaking drunk*)
bagnato fradicio	*soaking wet*
pieno zeppo	*packed out*

Language in action

Exercise 1

Interview with a commuter

– Dove abita, signor Ruzzini? Abita a Firenze?
– No, abito a Pisa, ma lavoro a Firenze.
– E viaggia ogni giorno?
– Sì. Prendo il treno tutti i giorni. Parto alle sette e arrivo alle otto. Comincio a lavorare alle 8.15.

Now write up the information supplied as a brief account of Signor Ruzzini's day:

Il signor Ruzzini comincia a lavorare alle 8.15 …

Exercise 2

Interview with a working mother

- Signora Giannini, a che ora comincia a lavorare?
- Comincio alle otto e trenta. Lavoro in centro.
- A che ora finisce?
- Finisco alle sette. Torno a casa stanca morta.
- E suo marito?
- Mio marito non lavora. Resta a casa con la bambina.
- E la sera?
- La sera guardiamo la tv.

Now write up this information in the form of a brief account:

La signora Giannini lavora in centro …

Exercise 3

Dialogue between friends

Carla   Vieni al cinema, Marco?
Marco   Sì, vengo volentieri.
Carla   Sbrigati, allora, stiamo uscendo proprio adesso.
Marco   Sto venendo. Mi sto mettendo le scarpe.
Carla   Sei sempre l'ultimo.
Marco   Stai scherzando! Tu sei la più lenta di tutti.

Highlight all the examples of **stare** and gerund. Now replace them by a normal present tense.

e.g. Sto mangiando > mangio.

Exercise 4

Although Nick is married to an Italian teacher and has spent a lot of time in Italy, he has never studied the language and has problems with the verbs. Sometimes he uses the infinitive form (**-are,** etc), sometimes he just misses them out altogether. Can you help him out by adding the appropriate verbs in his part of the conversation with his friend Gloria and making any other necessary changes?

G   Allora, Nick, dove andate in vacanza quest'anno?

N   Noi Argentina. Voi Sardegna come sempre?

G   Sì, si parte domani. E voi invece, quando partite?

N   Noi partire Oxford il 19 agosto di sera. Arrivare Buenos Aires il 20. E tornare Oxford il 5 settembre.

G   Come stanno i ragazzi?

N   Bene. Malcolm medicina a Cambridge, Alex ancora a scuola. Molta musica, molti amici, cinema la sera.

G   Ah, ho capito. Francesca frequenta l'Accademia di Brera, va tutti i giorni a Milano. E Anna?

N   Anna sempre al lavoro. A casa solo per la cena. Molto stressata. Finire libro di grammatica prima di settembre.

Exercise 5

Use **stare** and an appropriate gerund to say what you or someone else is doing. If you are already familiar with the object pronouns (see units 4 and 14*)*, use these too, where appropriate:

e.g. Gianna, cosa fai con quella maglietta? *(lavare)*
   Sto lavando la maglietta per stasera.
   La sto lavando. (Sto lavandola.)

  1   Loredana, cosa fai con la teiera?   *(preparare, fare un tè)*
  2   Gabriele, cosa fai con la patente?   *(andare a noleggiare la macchina)*
  3   Sabrina e Max, dove andate con il cane?   *(portare a spasso)*
  4   Giulio, cosa fai con la radio?   *(riparare)*
  5   Tania, cosa fai con tutta quella carta?   *(scrivere un romanzo)*
  6   Paolo, cosa fai con le forbici?   *(tagliare le unghie)*
  7   Nino, cosa fai con la valigia?   *(partire)*
  8   Camilla, cosa fai con la tazzina?   *(bere un caffè)*
  9   Eliana, cosa fai con la macchina fotografica?   *(fare una foto della nuova casa)*
 10   Dante, cosa fai al computer?   *(tradurre una lettera)*

TALKING ABOUT ROUTINE AND HABITS

Introduction

Study these short conversations about morning routine:

A che ora ti alzi, Gianna?	*What time do you get up, Gianna?*
Di solito mi alzo alle sei.	*Usually I get up at 6 a.m.*
Signora, a che ora si alza la mattina?	*What time do you get up in the morning, signora?*
Io mi alzo tardi, in genere verso le 8.00, e mi preparo un caffè.	*I get up, usually around 8 a.m., and make myself a coffee.*

Focus on grammar

1 Reflexive verbs

In Italian, verbs expressing actions one does to or for oneself are known
as reflexive verbs (verbs that refer back to the subject or person carrying
out the action). Many of them refer to everyday actions. Looking up the
verb in the dictionary you'll find it in its infinitive form (**-are**, **-ere**, or
-ire) with the final **e** dropped and the reflexive pronoun (**si**) attached to
the end:

alzare (*to get someone up*) + **si** = **alzarsi** (*to get oneself up*)
vestire (*to dress someone*) + **si** = **vestirsi** (*to dress oneself*)

To say what you do or what someone else does, you use the appropriate form of verb with the correct reflexive pronoun (**mi, ti, si**, etc.) (*myself, yourself, himself*, etc.) before the verb:

a) Reflexive verb forms

alzarsi (*to get up*)

mi alzo	*I get up*	**ci** alziamo	*we get up*
ti alzi	*you get up*	**vi** alzate	*you get up*
si alza	*he/she gets up*	**si** alzano	*they get up*
si alza	*you get up* (formal)		

Many of the verbs expressing this type of action are **-are** verbs, but there are **-ere** or **-ire** verbs as well, including some irregular verbs:

sedersi (*to sit down*)

mi siedo	*I sit down*	**ci** sediamo	*we sit down*
ti siedi	*you sit down*	**vi** sedete	*you sit down*
si siede	*he/she sits down*	**si** siedono	*they sit down*
si siede	*you sit down* (formal)		

vestirsi (*to dress*)

mi vesto	*I get dressed*	**ci** vestiamo	*we get dressed*
ti vesti	*you get dressed*	**vi** vestite	*you get dressed*
si veste	*he/she gets dressed*	**si** vestono	*they get dressed*
si veste	*you get dressed* (formal)		

b) Reflexive pronoun replacing the possessive

Frequently Italian uses the reflexive pronoun (**mi, ti**, etc.) where English would use the possessive (*my, your*, etc.) particularly when talking about articles of clothing or parts of the body. English says *I put my shoes on*, while Italian says *I put the shoes on myself*. It describes an action you carry out on yourself (or which someone else carries out on him/herself):

Mi metto **la** giacca per uscire.	*I put my jacket on to go out.*
Mia figlia **si** lava **i** capelli tutti i giorni.	*My daughter washes her hair every day.*

It can also describe an action one carries out *for* oneself:

Mi preparo **un** caffè.	*I'll make myself a coffee.*
Ti prepari **la** valigia?	*Are you packing your suitcase?*

In the cases above, the reflexive pronoun is not the direct object of the action as in **mi lavo** *(I wash myself)* but the indirect object **mi lavo i capelli** *(I wash the hair for myself)*. In the present tense, this makes no difference, but in the *passato prossimo* (perfect tense) whether the object is direct or indirect will determine whether the past participle agrees with the subject (see unit 11).

c) Reflexive infinitives: changing the pronoun

When using a verb, such as **devo** or **posso**, with an infinitive such as **truccarsi** (see unit 9 for more examples), remember that the reflexive pronoun will not always be **si** but will change according to the person it refers to:

truccarsi   *(to put on one's make-up)*

Devo truccar**mi** per andare alla festa.	*I must put on my make-up to go to the party.*

vestirsi   *(to get dressed)*

Bambini, **preferite** vestir**vi** da soli?	*Kids, do you prefer to get dressed by yourselves?*

prepararsi   *(to get ready)*

Perché ci metti tanto a preparar**ti**?	*Why do you take so long to get ready?*

Note: Ci used with **mettere** means *to take (time).*

2 Phrases of time

prima	*first*	più tardi	*later*
prima di me	*before me*	dopo	*after*
poi	*then*	alle tre	*at 3 o'clock*
verso le tre	*around, about 3 o'clock*		
dalle nove in poi	*from 9 o'clock on*		
dalle nove all'una	*from 9 to 1 o'clock*		
lunedì	*on Monday*		

3 Phrases expressing frequency

il lunedì	*every Monday*	spesso	*often*
ogni lunedì	*every Monday*	raramente	*rarely*
tutti i lunedì	*every Monday*	una volta	*once a month*
sempre	*always*	al mese	
di solito	*usually*	una volta	*once a day*
normalmente	*normally*	al giorno	
generalmente	*generally*	una volta	*once a year*
ogni tanto	*every so often*	all'anno	
qualche volta	*sometimes*	una volta	*once a week*
(non)... mai	*never*	alla settimana	

Language plus

1 Position of reflexive pronouns

Normally, the reflexive pronoun comes before the verb but in certain cases it follows and is joined to it.

a) with imperative forms

With the **tu, noi, voi** forms of the imperative, used for orders or commands (see unit 9), the reflexive pronoun is joined to the *end* of the verb:

Vi mettete le scarpe?	*Are you putting your shoes on?*
Mettete**vi** le scarpe.	*Put your shoes on!*
Ti metti il vestito nuovo?	*Are you putting your new dress on?*
Metti**ti** il vestito nuovo.	*Put your new dress on!*
Ci prepariamo.	*We're getting ready.*
Prepariamo**ci**.	*Let's get ready.*

b) with the gerund

Sto mettendo**mi** le scarpe.	*I'm putting my shoes on.*
Luisa sta truccando**si**.	*Luisa is putting her make-up on.*

c) with the infinitive

Vado a lavar**mi**.	*I'm going to wash.*
Cominciano a prepara**rsi**.	*They start to get ready.*

2 How to form adverbs

An adverb is similar in purpose to an adjective, but instead of describing a person or a thing, it describes the way someone does something, in other words it qualifies the verb.

Gli italiani guidano **velocemente**. *Italians drive fast.*

It can also describe extent or measure, and so is often found qualifying an adjective, or even another adverb. In the examples that follow, **troppo** and **molto** are adverbs:

Questa borsa è **troppo** grande.	*This bag is too big.*
Questo treno è **molto** veloce.	*This train is very fast.*
Tu guidi **troppo** velocemente.	*You drive too fast.*

There are two common ways in which adverbs are formed in Italian, and a few exceptions.

- Adjectives that end in **-o** such as **rapido, educato** change to the feminine form (rapid**a**) and add **-mente,** to become **rapidamente, educatamente**.
- Adjectives that end in **-e** such as **veloce**, add **-mente** to form adverbs such as **velocemente**. In the case of adjectives ending in **-le** or **-re** such as **facile, regolare**, the **e** is dropped first: **facilmente, regolarmente**.

The exceptions to these two rules include some common adjectives such as **buono** *(good)*, **cattivo** *(bad),* which have their own distinct adverbs: **bene** *(well)*, **male** *(badly).* (See Grammar Appendix 3.3 and 3.4.)

Often Italians prefer to use an adverbial phrase rather than an adverb, even if the adverb exists. Some examples are:

con attenzione	*with care, carefully*	senza cura	*without care, carelessly*
in modo educato	*in a polite way, politely*	in maniera sgarbata	*in an impolite way, rudely*

Lastly, it is quite common – especially in adverts – to find an adjective used instead of an adverb:

Mangiate **sano!** Mangiate Yoplait! *Eat healthily! Eat Yoplait!*
Chi va **piano** va **sano** e va **lontano**. *He who goes slowly goes safely and goes far.* (using *safe* rather than *safely)*

Language in action

Exercise 1

Getting ready

In the 'dialogue' below, highlight or underline the verbs used reflexively. Now continue giving the children orders, along these lines, using different verbs (see the list above in Exercise 1 for ideas). Alternatively, for a change, try giving orders to an imaginary partner, in the **tu** form.

Piero e Maddalena, perché non andate a farvi la doccia? Su, cercate di sbrigarvi! Poi mettetevi i vestiti puliti e pettinatevi un pochino. (Bevete il latte…)

Exercise 2

Say what you do first in the morning, using **preferire** and reflexive infinitives:

e.g. Ti fai prima la doccia o prendi il caffè?
Preferisco farmi prima la doccia.

1 Ti fai prima la doccia o ti vesti?
2 Ti metti prima i vestiti o prendi il caffè?
3 Ti metti prima le scarpe o i calzini?
4 Ti trucchi prima o ti pettini?
5 Ti lavi i capelli o ti vesti prima?
6 Ti lavi prima i denti o fai colazione?

Exercise 3

Use the example below as a basis to write an account of what you (and your friends or family) do every morning. Practise asking your partner (imaginary if necessary!) what they do in the morning. Use the 'time' words **prima, dopo** to say what order you do things in and use the verbs in the box.

A casa

La mattina mio marito si alza prima di me e mi prepara il caffè. Io mi alzo dopo, mi lavo, mi vesto e poi mi preparo ad uscire.

alzarsi   fare la doccia   farsi la barba.

preparare il caffè   fare colazione   lavarsi i capelli

lavarsi i denti   mettersi le scarpe   pettinarsi

svegliarsi   truccarsi   vestirsi

8 | TALKING ABOUT POSSIBILITY AND ASKING PERMISSION

Learn how to ...

■ Ask permission to do something ■ Ask someone if he/she is able to do something ■ Say you can or can't do something ■ Ask if something is allowed/possible

Language points

■ **Posso?** ■ **Può? mi può?** ■ Impersonal **si può? È possibile?**
■ **Sa, sa dirmi?**

Introduction

Study these examples of asking permission or asking if someone can do something:

Può indicarmi la strada per Pisa?	*Can you show me the way to Pisa?*
Posso telefonare da qui?	*Can I telephone from here?*
Si può parcheggiare?	*Can one park?*
È possibile telefonare?	*Is it possible to phone?*
Sa dirmi quanto costa?	*Can you tell me how much it costs?*

Focus on grammar

1 Potere

Potere means *to be able to (I can)*. It is an irregular verb, i.e. it does not follow the pattern of verbs we have seen so far. The forms of the present tense look like this:

posso	*I can*	possiamo	*we can*
puoi	*you can*	potete	*you can*
può	*he/she can*	possono	*they can*
	you can (formal)		

Potere is used to say what one is able, or not able, to do, to ask permission, or to ask other people if they can do something:

Non **posso** sopportare il caldo.	*I can't bear the heat.*
Possiamo prendere l'autobus?	*Can we get the bus?*
Non **posso** mangiare le fragole, perché sono allergica.	*I can't eat strawberries because I'm allergic (to them).*
Posso telefonare in Inghilterra?	*Can I phone England?*
Può cambiare questo biglietto da L.100.000?	*Can you change this L100,000 note?*
Può indicar**mi** la strada per Roma?	*Can you show me the road for Rome?*

There is an alternative way of asking the last question above, in which the pronoun is placed before the **può**:

Mi può indicare la strada per Roma?

2 Si può?

This is a way of asking if *one* can do something; it is general and does not mention a specific person:

Si può parcheggiare qui?	*Can one park here?*
Si può entrare?	*Can one come in?*
Si può telefonare in Inghilterra?	*Can one phone England?*

It can be replaced with the expression **È possibile?**:

È possibile parlare con il direttore?	*Is it possible to speak to the manager?*
È possibile andare in macchina?	*Is it possible to go by car?*

Language plus

1 Sapere

Sometimes the real meaning of *I can* is *I know how to* (**sapere**) and not *I can because circumstances permit* (**potere**):

So nuotare bene.	*I know how to swim well.*
	(I can swim well)
Sai cucinare?	*Can you cook?*

Sapere is also used to express the idea of knowing a piece of information:

Sai a che ora parte l'autobus?	*Do you know what time the bus leaves?*
Sa dirmi a che ora parte il treno?	*Can you tell me what time the train leaves?*

2 Omitting potere

In sentences where English uses *can,* the verb **potere** is often omitted in Italian:

Non sento niente.	*I can't hear anything.*
Non vediamo nessuno.	*We can't see anyone.*

3 Other tenses and moods of potere

Potere when used in the conditional mood (see unit 20) means *could*, for example:

Potresti farmi un favore?	*Could you do me a favour?*
Potrei passare domani.	*I could pass by tomorrow.*

Potere in the past conditional (see unit 21) means *could have:*

Avresti potuto avvertirmi.	*You could have warned me.*
Avrei potuto farne a meno.	*I could have done without it.*

Potere can be used in the *passato prossimo* (perfect) or the imperfect tense (see unit 11). If the sentence refers to one action or event, use the *passato prossimo*. If it is a continuing situation, where you would normally use the imperfect, then use this:

Non **ho potuto** telefonargli.	*I couldn't ring him.*
Non **potevo** aspettare. Avevo troppe cose da fare.	*I couldn't wait. I had too much to do.*

Potere normally takes **avere** in the *passato prossimo* but when followed by a verb taking **essere** it can use **essere** instead. In this case the past participle **(potuto)** has to agree with the subject in number and gender:

Non **sono potuto** venire.   *I couldn't come.*
  (Non **ho potuto** venire)
Non **siamo potuti** andare.   *We couldn't go.*
  (Non **abbiamo potuto** andare)

4 Other ways of saying 'to be able to'

a) *essere in grado di*

Essere in grado di means *to be able to, to be up to.* It is followed by the preposition **di**. Here are two examples:

Non **è in grado di** fare questo   *He is not up to this work.*
  lavoro.
Sei **in grado di** darmi una   *Are you able to give me a reply?*
  risposta?

b) *farcela*

Farcela is an idiomatic expression composed of **fare + ci + la,** meaning *to be able to, to manage to.* It is followed by the preposition **a**. Here are two examples:

Non ce la faccio più.   *I can't cope./ I can't go on./*
    I can't manage.

Ce la fai a portare quel tavolo?   *Can you manage to carry that table?*

5 Non ne posso più

Non ne posso più is an expression meaning *I can't bear it, I can't stand it any longer.*

Non ne possono più.   *They can't stand it any more.*

Language in action

Exercise 1

Passato prossimo or imperfect?

Read the Language Plus section then complete this exercise choosing the right past tense of **potere**:

Check the forms of the verb in the Verb List at the back of the book if necessary.

1   Scusa, non (*potere*) finire la traduzione, perché è arrivato mio cugino
    dall'Italia.
2   I nostri amici non (*potere*) andare in vacanza perché la bambina era
    malata.
3   Non (*potere*) venire al cinema perché avevo una lezione di pianoforte
    alle 5.00.
4   Non (*potere*) affittare la camera ad uno studente perché facevamo
    fare ancora i lavori in casa.
5   Io non (*potere*) vedere il film perché il cinema era chiuso.
6   Non (*potere*) uscire ieri sera perché eravamo senza soldi.

Exercise 2

Solving a problem

Suggest things your friend(s) might do, to solve their problems:

e.g. Come faccio ad arrivare in centro? Non ho la macchina. (*prendere
    l'autobus*)
    Potresti prendere l'autobus.

1   Gloria non ha niente da mettere.   (*comprare un vestito nuovo*)
2   Il marito di Giusy è ingrassato 20 kg.   (*stare a dieta*)
3   I ragazzi non sanno cosa fare stasera.   (*andare al cinema o rimanere
    a casa a studiare*)
4   Come si fa a conoscere ragazze inglesi?   (*andare al pub*)
5   Ho paura di essere bocciata in italiano.   (*studiare di più*)
6   Non abbiamo soldi per andare in vacanza con i nostri amici.   (*fare
    lo scambio di casa*)
7   Il governo vuole ridurre l'inquinamento nelle città.   (*vietare l'uso
    delle automobili*)
8. Non hai nessuna speranza di superare l'esame di storia
    contemporanea.   (*farmi aiutare da Marco*)

Exercise 3

Planning a holiday in Italy

Fleur and Tony are going to Tuscany for a short holiday. Their friend Maura helpfully tells them all the things they could see in Italy ... and all the things they could have seen had they organised their trip better! Fill in the gaps with the correct form of **potere**: the present, conditional, or past conditional (**avreste potuto**). (See Verb List at the end of the book.)

F   Vorremmo visitare Firenze, Pisa, Siena e Lucca in 5 giorni. ... vedere le chiese, i monumenti, magari anche qualche festa. Cosa ci consigli? Tony vorrebbe vedere il Palio e altre cose simili, mentre io preferisco visitare tutte le gallerie d'arte e i musei.

M   Eh ... sono troppe cose da vedere in poco tempo. Arrivate a Pisa e tornate d'a Pisa, vero? Peccato! (*Potere*) prendere un volo da Firenze per risparmiare tempo.

Comunque (*potere*) cominciare a Pisa, andare a vedere la Torre ... Poi Fleur (*potere*) visitare i musei, mentre tu, Tony, (*potere*) andare a vedere il Palio. Non so se riuscirai a trovare posto, ma (*potere*) provarci almeno.

(*Potere*) essere interessante anche fare una passeggiata lungo le mura antiche di Lucca. Poi da Lucca si (*potere*) prendere il pullman per Firenze ... è più veloce del treno. Se (*potere*), lasciate i bagagli alla stazione. Il centro di Firenze non è molto grande e si (*potere*) girare anche a piedi. In una giornata (*potere*) vedere i principali monumenti: il Duomo, Palazzo Pitti, il Ponte Vecchio. Se poi avete tempo, (*potere*) visitare anche San Lorenzo e la Cappella dei Medici.

Il giorno dopo, dovete tornare a Pisa per prendere l'aereo ... ma solo alle 16.00. Allora, Fleur (*potere*) approfittare delle ore libere per fare degli acquisti. Ci sono bellissimi negozi. Se vuoi, Tony, (*potere*) comprare qualcosa anche tu!

9 | GIVING ORDERS AND INSTRUCTIONS

Learn how to ...

■ Request, order or give instructions ■ Read written instructions
■ Tell someone not to do something

Language points

■ Imperative (command) form: **tu, Lei, noi, voi, loro** ■ Written
instructions using the infinitive ■ Negative forms of the imperative

Introduction

A command or order is expressed in Italian by a different verb form: the
imperative. Study these examples showing how the imperative form is
used to give orders or instructions:

Prendi un dolce, Marco!	*Have a cake, Marco.*
Mangia un panino!	*Eat a sandwich!*
Non fare complimenti!	*Don't hold back out of politeness!*
Senta! Scusi! Come arrivo alla stazione?	*Listen. Excuse me. How do I get to the station?*
Prenda Via Manzoni.	*Take Via Manzoni.*
Al primo semaforo giri a sinistra.	*At the first traffic lights turn left.*
Non giri a destra!	*Don't turn right.*
Andiamo al cinema!	*Let's go to the cinema!*
C'è un film di Troisi.	*There's a Troisi film.*
Non facciamo tardi.	*Let's not be late.*

Bambini, andate a giocare in giardino!	*Children, go and play in the garden!*
Non andate fuori scalzi, mettetevi le scarpe!	*Don't go out with bare feet, put your shoes on!*
Signorine, si accomodino!	*Ladies, please sit down!*
Non si preoccupino!	*Don't worry!*
Aprire con cautela.	*Open with care. (Instructions on a packet)*

Focus on grammar

1 Imperative (tu form)

When giving an instruction to someone you are on friendly terms with, use the **tu** form. The ending is **-a** for the **-are** verbs or **-i** for the **-ere** and **-ire** verbs (the same as the normal **tu** form of these verbs):

Parlare	**Parla** chiaro!	*Speak clearly!*
Prendere	**Prendi** qualcosa da mangiare!	*Have something to eat!*
Sentire	**Senti** questo!	*Listen to this!*
Pulire	**Pulisci** la bocca!	*Wipe your mouth!*

2 Imperative (Lei form)

When giving an order to someone you are on formal terms with, use the **Lei** (formal *you*) form. For the **-are** verbs the imperative ends in **-i**; for **-ere** and **-ire** verbs it ends in **-a**:

Portare	Mi **porti** il menù!	*Bring me the menu!*
Prendere	**Prenda** un biscotto!	*Take a biscuit!*
Sentire	**Senta!**	*Listen!*
Finire	**Finisca** pure!	*Do finish!*

3 Imperative (noi form)

Not exactly a command, the **noi** form is a way of exhorting one's friends to do something when the speaker himself/herself is part of the group. The form of the imperative is the same as the normal **noi** form of the present tense:

Parlare	**Parliamo** italiano!	*Let's talk Italian!*
Prendere	**Prendiamo** un gelato!	*Let's have an ice-cream!*
Sentire	**Sentiamo** cosa vuole.	*Let's hear what he wants!*
Finire	**Finiamo** domani!	*Let's finish tomorrow!*

4 Imperative (voi form)

This is the form of imperative or order normally used when addressing more than one person (the polite **loro** form exists but is seldom used). The form is exactly the same as the normal **voi** form of the present tense:

Giocare	**Giocate** in giardino, bambini!	*Play in the garden, children!*
Mettere	**Mettete** le ciabatte, ragazzi!	*Put your flip-flops on, kids!*
Dormire	**Dormite** bene, ragazzi!	*Sleep well, kids!*
Finire	**Finite** i compiti!	*Finish your homework!*

5 Imperative (loro form)

Loro (the formal plural *you* form) is sometimes used by shop assistants, waiters, hotel employees, etc. when addressing more than one customer. You are unlikely to need to use it yourself unless planning on spending a working summer in Italy. The first two examples shown are of reflexive verbs:

Accomodarsi **Si accomodino!**	*Please make yourselves comfortable!*
	(Please sit down, come in)
Sedersi	**Si siedano!**	*Please sit down.*
Dormire	**Dormano** bene, signori!	*Sleep well!*
Finire	**Finiscano** pure di mangiare, signori! Non c'è fretta.
	Do finish eating, there's no hurry.

6 Giving instructions (using the infinitive)

Recipes, instruction manuals and other written instructions often use the infinitive (the 'to' form of the verb):

Tagliare la cipolla e **mettere** in un tegame.

Chop the onion and place in a frying pan.

Moderare la velocità!

Reduce your speed!

How to make a telephone call (Instructions in phone booth)

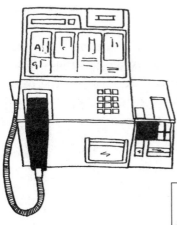

Staccare il ricevitore, e **inserire** le monete. **Comporre** il numero. Alla fine della telefonata **riattaccare** il ricevitore e **attendere** la restituzione delle monete.

7 Telling someone not to do something

For the **Lei**, **noi**, **voi** or **loro** forms, add **non** before the verb:

Non esca, signora!

Don't go out, signora!

Non andiamo da Maria!

Let's not go to Maria's!

Non girate a sinistra!

Don't turn left!

Non si preoccupino!

Don't worry!

But for the **tu** form, use **non** and the infinitive form (the **-are, -ere, -ire** form):

Non mangiare troppo!	*Don't eat too much!*
Non prendere tutto!	*Don't take all (of it)!*
Non dormire fino a tardi!	*Don't sleep in!*

Non is also added to instructions given in the infinitive:

Non parlare al conducente!   *Don't speak to the driver!*

Language plus

1 Irregular imperatives

Many verbs have an imperative form which does not follow the form shown above. Some of the most common irregular imperative forms are:

Infinitive		tu	Lei	voi	Loro
andare	*(to go)*	va'	vada	andate	vadano
fare	*(to do)*	fa'	faccia	fate	facciano
stare	*(to be)*	sta'	stia	state	stiano
dare	*(to give)*	da'	dia	date	diano
dire	*(to say)*	di'	dica	dite	dicano
essere	*(to be)*	sii	sia	siate	siano
avere	*(to have)*	abbi	abbia	abbiate	abbiano

The **Lei** form of the imperative is the 3rd person (*he, she, you*) of the present subjunctive, a verb form used only in specific circumstances (see unit 17). See Verb list for the subjunctive forms of irregular verbs.

The one-syllable imperatives shown above are often spelt differently: **va, fà, sta, dà, dì**. Perhaps because they sound so abrupt, there is a tendency for the first four to be replaced by the normal non-imperative **tu** forms: **vai, fai, stai, dai**.

2 Pronouns – before or after?

See Grammar Appendix (4.3).

Language in action

Exercise 1

Cosa c'è da vedere a Napoli?

One of your friends is going to Naples soon, with his girlfriend. Tell him what to go and see and give him some advice on where and what to eat, where to stay, how to get around. Use the basic information supplied below. Try not to use **andare** all the time, here are some other ideas: **assaggiare, bere, cercare, comprare, fare, mangiare, prendere, prenotare, provare, stare, visitare.**

Da vedere
- Castello dell'Ovo
- Palazzo Reale
- Museo nazionale
- Chiostri di Santa Chiara

Da comprare
- Figurine per il presepe (San Gregorio Armeno)
- Vestiti (Via Toledo o Vomero)
- Corallo
- Articoli di pelle

Da mangiare e bere
- Limoncello
- Sfogliatelle napoletane
- Pizza
- Pesce

Dove alloggiare
- Continental (Via Partenope)
- Bella Napoli (Via Caracciolo)
- Majestic (Largo Vasto a Chiaia)
- Terminus (vicino alla stazione ferroviaria)

Fuori città
- Posillipo (autobus)
- Pompei (la Circumvesuviana)
- Capri (aliscafo o nave)
- Sorrento (la Circumvesuviana)

e.g. Vai a vedere i chiostri di Santa Chiara. Cerca di …

Exercise 2

Come si arriva a ...?

Read this dialogue in which a tourist is given directions by a student:

Turista	**Senta, scusi!** Come arrivo alla stazione?
Studente	Dunque ... **vada** diritto per questa strada, al primo semaforo **giri** a sinistra, **continui** ancora un po', e in fondo a quella strada **volti** a destra ... **attraversi** la piazza e la stazione è proprio di fronte.
Turista	Ah, grazie. Lei è molto gentile.

Now make up your own dialogue in which you explain to a visiting Italian tourist how to arrive at the Bodleian Library (**Biblioteca Bodleiana**), Oxford, from the Museum of Oxford. Use the map opposite:

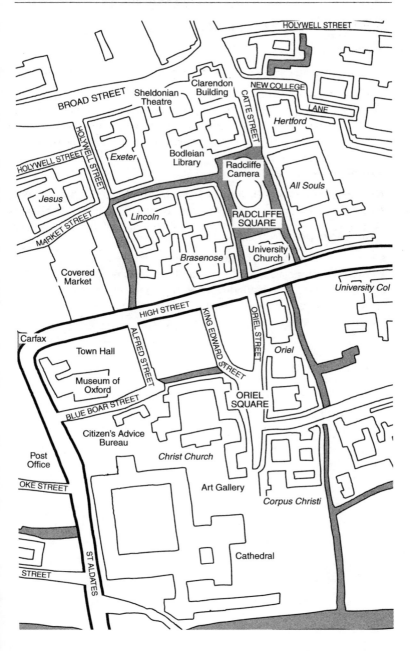

10 TALKING ABOUT POSSESSION

Learn how to ...

■ Ask to whom something belongs ■ Say to whom something belongs
■ Ask what other people have/own

Language points

■ Possessive adjectives **mio, tuo, suo, nostro, vostro, loro**
■ Possessive pronouns **mio, il mio**, etc; Possessive **proprio**
■ Using reflexive pronoun/indirect object pronoun instead of possessive ■ **di** expressing ownership; **Di chi è?** ■ **avere** expressing ownership ■ **Quale** to ask which item belongs to someone

Introduction

First look at these examples of possessives **mio, tuo,** etc:

La tua casa è grande.	*Your house is big.*
La mia è piccola.	*Mine is small.*
È tua questa giacca?	*Is this jacket yours?*
No, non è mia.	*No. It's not mine.*
Di chi è questa bicicletta?	*Whose is this bike?*
È di Franco.	*It's Franco's.*
Lei ha una macchina inglese?	*Do you have an English car?*
No, ho una macchina tedesca.	*No. I have a German car.*
Qual è la Sua macchina?	*Which is your car?*
Quella verde.	*That green one.*
Qual è il Suo indirizzo?	*What is your address?*

Focus on grammar

1 Mio, tuo, suo, *etc.*

To say to whom something belongs in Italian, use **mio, tuo, suo,** etc. (*my, your, his*, etc.); these are possessive adjectives. Like all adjectives, **mio, tuo, suo, nostro, vostro** change according to whether the person or thing they are describing is singular or plural, masculine or feminine.

Unlike English, Italian uses the definite article **il, la,** etc. with possessives (**il mio cane, la mia macchina**).

However when talking about relatives, you don't need the definite article, unless there is more than one relative or unless there is an adjective or suffix: **mio padre, mia cugina** *but* **i miei fratelli, la mia sorellina, il mio fratello più grande**.

a) *mio* (my)

il mio cane *my dog*	**mia** madre *my mother*
mio padre *my father*	**i miei** jeans *my jeans*
la mia bicicletta *my bicycle*	**le mie** sorelle *my sisters*

b) *tuo* (your)

Use **tuo** when speaking informally to someone (**tu** form):

il tuo passaporto (*your passport*)	**la tua** amica (*your friend*)
i tuoi figli (*your children*)	**le tue** scarpe (*your shoes*)

c) *suo* (his, her)

Suo means *his* or *her*:

il suo amico (*his/her friend*)	**la sua** collega (*his/her colleague*)
i suoi amici (*his/her friends*)	**le sue** cose (*his/her things*)

Suo can also mean *your* (when using the polite **Lei** form); with this meaning, it is often written with capital **S** just as the **Lei** form is often written with a capital **L**:

    È arrivato **Suo** marito?   *Has your husband arrived?*

d) His or her?

Sometimes when **suo** is used, it is not clear whether it means *his* or *her.*

Look at this sentence:

Ho visto Giorgio stasera.	*I saw Giorgio tonight. He was*
Era con Sandra. **Il suo** amico	*with Sandra.* **His/Her** *friend*
era appena tornato da Londra.	*had just got back from London.*

To avoid confusion between *his* and *her*, you can if necessary replace **suo** – or add to it – by the words **di lui** (*of him*) or **di lei** (*of her*):

Ho visto Giorgio oggi. Era con	*I saw Giorgio today. He was*
Sandra. L'amico **di lei** era appena	*with Sandra.* **Her** *friend had*
tornato da Londra.	*just got back from London.*

e) *nostro* (our)

il nostro treno *(our train)*	**la nostra** amica *(our friend)*
i nostri mariti *(our husbands – one each)*	**le nostre** case *(our houses)*

f) *vostro* (your)

Use **vostro** when referring to more than one person:

il vostro errore *(your mistake)*	**la vostra** macchina fotografica *(your camera)*
i vostri biglietti *(your tickets)*	**le vostre** valigie *(your suitcases)*

g) *loro* (their)

Loro is an exception to the rules above, because it never changes whatever the gender or number of the object or person it describes and it *always* takes the definite article (**il, la**, etc.).

il loro cane *(their dog)*	**la loro** casa *(their house)*
i loro amici *(their friends)*	**le loro** cose *(their things)*

Loro can also mean *your* when addressing people using the formal plural form **loro,** but this use is really limited to waiters, hotel staff, etc. addressing clients.

2 il mio, il tuo, il suo, *etc.*

To express ownership without naming the object, use the possessive pronouns **il mio, il tuo, il suo** (*mine, yours, his/hers*) etc. rather than the adjective **mio** (*my*). The article **il, lo, la**, etc. and the form of **mio, tuo, suo, nostro, vostro** still have to agree with the object or person owned, both in gender (masculine or feminine) and number (singular or plural):

Questo libro è **nostro.**	*This book is ours.*
Il vostro dov'è?	*Where's yours?*
Il nostro è in macchina.	*Ours is in the car.*
Mio marito mi aiuta molto in cucina.	*My husband helps me a lot in the kitchen.*
Il mio non sa dov'è.	*Mine doesn't know where it is.*
Di chi è questa felpa?	*Whose is that sweatshirt?*
È **mia. La tua** è più sporca.	*It's mine. Yours is dirtier.*

When the possessive is used with **essere** alone, as in the examples below, the definite article (**il,** etc.) is often omitted. One of the first phrases Italian children learn is **È mio!** (*It's mine!*)

Di chi è questo libro?	È **mio.**	*It's mine.*
Di chi è questa borsa?	È **tua.**	*It's yours.*
Di chi è questa macchina?	È **sua.**	*It's his.*
Di chi sono questi sandali?	Sono **nostri.**	*They're ours.*
	Sono **vostri.**	*They're yours.*
But ...	Sono **i loro.**	*They're theirs.*

Whether or not the article (**il, la**, etc.) is used, **mio, tuo, suo** still change according to whether the object is masculine or feminine, singular or plural.

The phrase **i tuoi** used without any noun often means *your family,* while **i miei** means *my family* and so on ...

3 Proprio

Proprio means *one's own* and is used in place of the other possessive adjectives when the subject referred to is an impersonal one, for example *one* or *everyone*:

Non tutti hanno **la propria** macchina. *Not everyone has their own car.*
Ognuno ama **il proprio** paese.   *Everyone loves his own country.*

It can, however, also be used with one of the other possessives, to reinforce or emphasise the idea of *one's own*:

| Marco è contento di vivere **la sua propria** vita. | *Marco is happy to live his own life.* |

4 Di *expressing ownership*

The English phrase *It's Franco's* has to be expressed in Italian by using **di** *(of)* followed by the person's name:

Questa maglia è **di** Franco.	*This sweater is Franco's.*
Queste scarpe sono **di** Anna.	*These shoes are Anna's.*

To ask who something belongs to, use **di** *(of)* and **chi** *(who)*:

Di chi è questa borsetta?	*Whose is this handbag?*
È **di** Cristina.	*It's Cristina's.*
Di chi sono questi soldi?	*Whose is this money?*
Sono **di** Filippo.	*It's Filippo's.*

5 Del, della, *etc.*

If instead of a person's name, there is a noun such as **ragazzo** or **amico**, the **di** combines with the definite article **il, la** (etc.) to create the forms **del, dello, dell', della**. All the forms of **del,** both singular and plural, are illustrated in unit 3 (used to express *some*).

Di chi è questa bicicletta?	*Whose is this bicycle?*
È **del** mio amico.	*It's my friend's.*
Di chi sono queste scarpe?	*Whose are these shoes?*
Sono **della** ragazza francese.	*They're the French girl's.*
Di chi sono questi asciugamani?	*Whose are these towels?*
Sono **dell'**albergo.	*They're the hotel's.*
Di chi sono questi libri?	*Whose are these books?*
Sono **dello** studente inglese.	*They're the English student's.*

Language plus

1 *Omission of possessive*

Italians tend to omit the possessive where the idea of ownership or possession is taken for granted:

Carla è partita con **il marito**.   *Carla left with her husband.*
(It is assumed that Carla left with her own husband)

I bambini hanno alzato **le mani**.   *The children raised their hands.*
(It is assumed that they raised their own hands)

È arrivato **lo zio**.   *Uncle's arrived.*
(Again, it is thought unnecessary to add whose uncle it is)

2 Using reflexive or indirect object pronoun

Italian frequently uses a pronoun where English would use a possessive. The reflexive pronoun is used to refer to one's own body or belongings.

Mi metto le scarpe.   *I put my shoes on.*

See unit 7 for more examples.

The *indirect object* pronoun is used to refer to someone else or someone else's belongings and is often used when doing something to or for someone else:

Vuoi che **ti** stiri la camicia?   *Do you want me to iron your shirt?*
Mamma, Aurelio **mi** ha tirato   *Mamma, Aurelio pulled my hair!*
 i capelli!

4 Omitting 'of' with possessive

Italian omits *of* in the following expressions:

due miei amici   *two of my friends*
un mio amico   *a friend of mine*

5 Verb avere expressing ownership

Avere (*to have*) can be used to talk about possessions. See Grammar appendix, list of irregular verbs.

Ha un cane, signor Bianchi?   *Do you have a dog, signor Bianchi?*
Sì. Si chiama Lillo.   *Yes. He is called Lillo.*

6 Quale

Quale means *which*. In unit 5 you saw **quale** used as an adjective.

Quale borsa vuole?   *Which bag do you want?*

You can also use it on its own when asking for information (such as someone's particulars) where in English you would use *what*. Before **è** *(it is)* it can be abbreviated but should *not* be followed by an apostrophe:

Singular

Qual è il Suo cognome?   *What is your surname?*

Qual è la tua data di nascita?	*What is your date of birth?*
Qual è la tua macchina?	*Which is your car?*

Plural

Quali sono i tuoi figli?	*Which are your children?*
Quali sono le tue scarpe?	*Which are your shoes?*
Quali sono i tuoi amici più cari?	*Who are your closest friends?*

Language in action

Exercise 1

Chi sono?

Francesco is talking about his family. Can you work out from the family tree (on p. 80) who everyone is? Fill in the gaps with the answers, including their relationship to Francesco and the correct possessive adjective:

Allora, questo è .... Marco. Questa è .... Marina, e questi sono .... Carlotta e Simone. Questa, invece, è .... Irma, con .... Ugo, e .... Flavia e Diana. .... casa è vicino alla nostra. Ugo quindi è .... e Flavia e Diana sono .... E questo è .... cane che dorme nella stanza di Flavia.

Exercise 2

Complete these sentences with the correct form of the verb (present or past), and reflexive pronoun.

e.g. Bambini, (*mettersi*) le scarpe.
    Bambini, **mettetevi** le scarpe.

1   Aspettami. Devo solo (*mettersi*) la giacca.
2   Ho freddo. (*Mettersi*) un maglione.
3   Ieri pioveva. Per uscire, (*mettersi*) un impermeabile e ho preso un ombrello.
4   Hai il braccio ingessato! Che (*farsi*)?
5   Sono caduto dalla bici e (*rompersi*) il polso.
6   Alessandro (*portarsi*) via il computer. Ne aveva bisogno per scrivere il tema.
7   Era il compleanno di mia madre. (*Mangiarsi*) tutta una scatola di cioccolatini in una sera.
8   Fa caldo qui dentro. (*Togliersi*) la maglia altrimenti sarai tutta sudata.

11 | TALKING ABOUT EVENTS AND ACTIONS IN THE PAST

Learn how to ...

■ Talk about events and actions in the past ■ Talk about events in the past relating to the present ■ Talk about events still going on

Language points

■ Perfect tense (**passato prossimo**) and **avere** ■ Perfect tense and **essere** ■ Verbs which can take both **essere** and **avere** in the perfect tense ■ Phrases of time past ■ Reflexive verbs in the perfect tense ■ Negative sentences in the perfect tense ■ Use of present tense with **da** ■ Months and days ■ Historic past tense (**passato remoto**)

Introduction

Look at these sentences referring to past events or actions:

Sabato sono andato al mare e ho mangiato un gelato. E tu dove sei stato?*	*On Saturday I went to the seaside and I ate an ice-cream. And where did you go?*
Siamo stati in America per 10 anni.	*We were in America for 10 years.*
Vivo in Inghilterra da 10 anni.	*I have lived in England for 10 years.*
Non lo vedo da cinque giorni.	*I haven't seen him for five days.*
Hai mai visto una casa così brutta?	*Have you ever seen such an ugly house?*
Cristoforo Colombo scoprì l'America nel 1492.	*Christopher Columbus discovered America in 1492.*

*stare (*to be*) in this context is similar in meaning to the verb **andare** (*to go*).

Focus on grammar

1 Perfect tense (passato prossimo)

In the examples above the *passato prossimo* (perfect tense) is used. It is used when talking about an action which is now over (finished, perfect) but has some connection with present events. The *passato prossimo* can translate the English perfect tense, e.g. *I have eaten* or the past definite, e.g. *I ate* in all the contexts listed below:

a) No specific occasion mentioned:

    Sei mai stato in Italia?   *Have you ever been to Italy?*

b) A specific occasion or time mentioned:

    Sì. Ci **sono stato due anni fa.**   *Yes. I went there two years ago.*

c) An action which took place over a longer period of time but is complete:

    Siamo vissuti a Roma **per 10 anni.** *We lived in Rome for 10 years.*

2 Perfect tense with avere

To form the *passato prossimo*, you use the present tense of the verb **avere** *(to have)* with the past participle **mangiato, dormito, venduto,** etc. *(eaten, slept, sold,* etc.). The verb **avere** changes according to *who* carried out the action: **ho, hai, ha,** etc., while the participle does not change:

    Ho mangiato un gelato.   *I ate/ have eaten an ice-cream.*
    Abbiamo dormito per due ore. *We slept / have slept for two hours.*

Here is the *passato prossimo* of the verb **mangiare** *(to eat)*:

ho	mangiato	**abbiamo**	mangiato
hai	mangiato	**avete**	mangiato
ha	mangiato	**hanno**	mangiato

3 Forms of past participle

In Italian the participles of all **-are** verbs have a regular form **-ato**:

| mangiare *(to eat)* | **ho mangiato** | *I have eaten, I ate* |
| parlare *(to speak)* | **ho parlato** | *I have spoken, I spoke* |

The participle of the **-ire** verbs is always **-ito**:

| dormire *(to sleep)* | **ho dormito** | *I have slept, I slept* |

But the participle of the **-ere** verbs can take any one of a number of forms. It might take an **-uto** form, for example:

| dovere *(to have to)* | **ho dovuto** | *I had to* |

Or it might take a shorter form such as:

| mettere *(to put)* | **ho messo** | *I have put, I put* |

There is no rule to help you learn all these forms, you just have to remember them! Here are **avere** and **essere** along with some of the more common **-ere** verbs, and their past participles:

avere	*to have*	**avuto**
essere	*to be*	**stato***
chiudere	*to close*	**chiuso**
decidere	*to decide*	**deciso**
dovere	*to have to*	**dovuto**
leggere	*to read*	**letto**
perdere	*to lose*	**perso, perduto**
potere	*to be able to*	**potuto**
prendere	*to take*	**preso**
rimanere	*to remain*	**rimasto***
rispondere	*to reply*	**risposto**
scendere	*to get down*	**sceso***
scrivere	*to write*	**scritto**
tenere	*to hold*	**tenuto**
vedere	*to see*	**visto**
vivere	*to live*	**vissuto*** (optional)
volere	*to want to*	**voluto**

The participles marked with an asterisk (*) are those that can form the *passato prossimo* with **essere** instead of **avere**. See below.

4 *Perfect tense with* essere

■ Agreement of past participle

Some verbs use **essere** *(to be)* with the past participle, instead of **avere** *(to have)*. In this case, the past participle changes its ending depending on whether the subject (the person or thing that has carried out the action) is masculine or feminine, singular or plural:

Carlo **è andato** in banca.	*Carlo has gone to the bank.*
Anna **è andata** al bar.	*Anna has gone to the café.*
Mario e Maria **sono andati** a scuola.	*Mario and Maria have gone to school.*
Daniela e Franca **sono andate** al cinema.	*Daniela and Franca have gone to the cinema.*

There are several verbs which use **essere** rather than **avere**. Most of these verbs are intransitive, in other words they do not take an object.

■ Transitive or intransitive verb?

Try asking the question 'what' after the verb. If it makes sense, then the verb is transitive (takes an object). If it does not make sense, then the verb is intransitive (does *not* take an object). For example, **Mario parte**. The question **parte ... che cosa?** does not make sense. **Partire** cannot take an object, so it is intransitive and takes **essere**. **Mario parla**. **Parla ... cosa?** Clearly the question can be answered: **Mario parla italiano**. So **parlare** is transitive and takes **avere**.

■ Which verbs take *essere*?

Verbs taking **essere** can be summarised as follows:

a) *essere, stare*

essere *(to be)*	**sono stato/a**
stare *(to be)*	**sono stato/a**

Sono stata in chiesa stamattina.

b) Verbs of movement or non-movement

andare	*(to go)*	arrivare	*(to arrive)*
cadere	*(to fall)*	entrare	*(to enter)*
partire	*(to leave, depart)*	restare	*(to stay behind,*
rimanere	*(to remain, stay behind)*		*to remain)*
scappare	*(to run off, escape)*	salire	*(to go up)*
tornare	*(to return)*	scendere	*(to go down)*
venire	*(to come)*	uscire	*(to go out)*

Il bambino **è caduto** dall'albero. *The child fell from a tree.*
Gli ospiti **sono venuti** alle 8.00. *The guests came at 8 p.m.*

c) Verbs expressing physical or other change

apparire *(to appear)*	crescere *(to grow)*
dimagrire *(to get thin)*	divenire *(to become)*
diventare *(to become)*	ingrassare *(to get fat)*
invecchiare *(to grow old)*	morire *(to die)*
nascere *(to be born)*	scomparire *(to disappear)*

Mia madre **è dimagrita** di 5 kg. *My mother lost 5 kgs.*
Io **sono ingrassata** di 2kg. *I put on 2 kgs.*
Sono morto di fame. *I'm starving (dead with hunger).*
  (not always literally)
Sono nata il 14 ottobre. *I was born on 14 October.*

d) Verbs that are impersonal or used impersonally ('it' verbs)

accadere *(to happen)*	avvenire *(to happen)*
bastare *(to be enough)*	capitare *(to happen)*
convenire *(to suit)*	costare *(to cost)*
dispiacere *(to displease)*	mancare *(to be lacking)*
parere *(to appear)*	piacere *(to please)*
sembrare *(to seem)*	servire *(to be useful for)*
succedere *(to happen)*	valere *(to be worth)*
volerci *(to take time)*	

Quanto è **costato**?	*How much did it cost?*
Ti è **piaciuto** il film?	*Did you like the film?*
Mi è **sembrato** stanco.	*He seemed tired to me.*
Ci è **voluta** un'ora.	*It took an hour.*

See unit 18 for details on impersonal verbs.

e) Verbs describing weather:

nevicare *(to snow)*	piovere *(to rain)*

Ieri è **piovuto** tantissimo.	*Yesterday it rained a lot.*

In spoken Italian, these verbs can also be used with **avere**.

5 Perfect tense with either essere or avere

Some verbs can be either transitive or intransitive. These verbs take **essere** or **avere** depending on their meaning. When they are transitive (do take an object, even if not explicit), they use **avere**. When they are intransitive (do not take an object) they use **essere**:

aumentare *(to increase)*	finire *(to finish)*
cominciare *(to begin)*	migliorare *(to improve)*
continuare *(to continue)*	passare *(to pass, pass by)*
diminuire *(to decrease)*	scendere *(to descend, come down)*

Ho passato il menù a Luca.	*I passed the menu to Luca.*
Sono passata da Gianluca.	*I went by Gianluca's.*
Hanno sceso le scale.	*They came down the stairs.*
Sono scesi per le scale.	*They came down by the stairs.*
Sono scesi dalla macchina.	*They got out of the car.*
I miei figli **hanno cominciato** le vacanze ieri.	*My kids began their holidays yesterday.*
Le vacanze **sono cominciate** ieri.	*The holidays began yesterday.*
Abbiamo finito gli esami una settimana fa.	*We finished the exams a week ago.*
Gli esami **sono finiti** la settimana scorsa.	*The exams finished last week.*

6 Perfect tense of reflexive verbs

Reflexive verbs (see unit 7) in the perfect tense need **essere**. The reflexive pronoun *(myself, yourself,* etc.) normally comes before the verb, although a reflexive verb in the infinitive has the **-si** tacked on to the end:

alzarsi	*to get up*	mi sono alzato
sedersi	*to sit down*	mi sono seduto
vestirsi	*to get dressed*	mi sono vestito

As with the other verbs that use **essere**, the participle (**alzato, vestito**, etc.) has to agree with the subject (masculine or feminine, singular or plural):

Giuliano **si è alzato** alle sette. *Giuliano got up at 7.00.*
Maria Grazia **si è alzata** alle otto. *Maria Grazia got up at 8.00*
I ragazzi **si sono alzati** tardi. *The boys got up late.*
Le bambine **si sono alzate** presto. *The girls got up early.*

7 Expressions of past time

To say how long ago you did something you use **fa** *(ago)* and the appropriate length of time:

due giorni **fa**	*two days ago*	un anno **fa**	*a year ago*
una settimana **fa**	*a week ago*	poco tempo **fa**	*a short time ago*
un mese **fa**	*a month ago*	pochi giorni **fa**	*a few days ago*

To talk about the past few days or weeks we use **scorso**:

la settimana **scorsa**	*last week*	l'anno **scorso**	*last year*
il mese **scorso**	*last month*	l'estate **scorsa**	*last summer*

Here are some common time phrases referring to the past:

ieri	*yesterday*	stamattina	*this morning*
l'altro ieri	*the day before yesterday*	ieri mattina	*yesterday morning*
oggi	*today*	ieri sera	*yesterday evening*

And the days of the week are as follows:

lunedì	*Monday*	venerdì	*Friday*
martedì	*Tuesday*	sabato	*Saturday*
mercoledì	*Wednesday*	domenica	*Sunday*
giovedì	*Thursday*		

The months of the year:

gennaio	*January*	luglio	*July*
febbraio	*February*	agosto	*August*
marzo	*March*	settembre	*September*
aprile	*April*	ottobre	*October*
maggio	*May*	novembre	*November*
giugno	*June*	dicembre	*December*

8 Negative past sentences

When the sentence in the perfect tense is negative, take care over the positioning of **non** and the other negative words. Italian negatives usually come in pairs (this is called a double negative) with **non** before the verb and the other negative word somewhere after. Look at some examples.

Here the second negative comes after **avere** or **essere** but before the participle:

Non sono **mai** stata a Palermo.   *I have never been to Palermo.*
Non abbiamo **ancora** mangiato.   *We haven't eaten yet.*

Here the second negative word comes after the *whole* verb:

Non ho visto **nessuno** oggi.   *I haven't seen anyone today.*
Non ho fatto **niente** ieri.   *I didn't do anything yesterday.*

For further examples of negative words, see the Grammar Appendix (9).

9 Present tense with da

When the event in question is still going on, use the present tense with **da**:

Studio l'italiano **da** 5 anni.   *I have been studying Italian for 5 years.*
   (Lit: I study Italian since 5 years.)

Sono sposata **da** 10 anni.   *I have been married for 10 years.*
Non la **vedo da** tanto tempo.   *I haven't seen her for so long.*

Language plus

1 The historic past (passato remoto)

As we saw above, the perfect tense *(passato prossimo)* is the tense generally used in spoken Italian when talking about an action in the past, especially if it is somehow related to the present context:

Non **ho** ancora **mangiato**.   *I haven't eaten yet.*
Ieri **è andata** in centro e **ha**   *Yesterday she went to the (town)*
  comprato una maglia.   *centre and bought a sweater.*

But speakers in the south will sometimes use the historic past *(passato remoto)* which is only used in the rest of Italy to describe a historic event (e.g. the Romans invading Britain) or a completed action in the past with no link to the present day. Here is an example of how the past historic might be used in written Italian:

Maria Stuarda **nacque** nel 1542, **sposò** giovane il futuro Re di
  Francia e **morì** decapitata nel 1587 per ordine della Regina
  Elisabetta d'Inghilterra.
Mary Queen of Scots was born in 1542, married very young the
  future King of France and died beheaded in 1587 by order of
  Elizabeth Queen of England.

Although it is unlikely that you will want to use the *passato remoto* (also known as the past absolute or past definite) its forms are supplied in the Grammar Appendix (13.1).

2 Subject pronouns io, tu, lui, etc.

The subject pronouns **io, tu, lui,** etc. are used to emphasise or contrast two different actions by two different people:

Io ho telefonato.   *I phoned.*
Lui non ha telefonato.   *He didn't phone.*
Io sono stata ad Assisi ma **tu** non   *I have been to Assisi but you*
  ci sei mai stata.   *have never been there.*

Language in action

Exercise 1

Le vacanze di Claudia

Read this dialogue between Claudia and Gianna, in which Claudia tells Gianna all about their recent holidays in the country. It didn't please everyone! Try and fill in the gaps in their conversation, using the *passato prossimo* of the verbs supplied and making any necessary changes:

Gianna   Bentornati dalle vacanze! Come *(andare)*? Tutto bene? Cosa *(fare)* di bello?

Claudia Sì, *(essere)* una vacanza un po' diversa dal solito... non *(andare)* al mare quest'anno, *(prendere)* una casa in campagna.

Gianna   E cosa *(fare)* in campagna?

Claudia Io *(fare)* delle lunghe passeggiate, Giovanni *(leggere)* molti libri, e non *(vedere)* nessuno. *(Mangiare)*, *(cucinare)* e *(dormire)*.

Gianna   E i bambini? *(Divertirsi)*?

Claudia No. I bambini *(lamentarsi)* perché per tre settimane non *(potere)* guardare la televisione. *(Giocare)* a pallone, *(andare)* in giro in bicicletta, e ci *(aiutare)* a preparare da mangiare.

Notes:

La passeggiata: This also refers to the nightly promenade up and down the main street, piazza, or sea front to be seen in any Italian town.

di bello, di speciale – note the following expressions:

qualcosa **di bello**	*something nice*
qualcosa **di buono**	*something nice (to eat)*
niente **di speciale**	*nothing special*

Exercise 2

Le Vacanze di Claudia (bis)

Now write an account of Claudia's holiday in Italian, in the third person, using all the facts contained in the dialogue:

e.g. Claudia e suo marito Giovanni hanno passato le vacanze in campagna ...

Exercise 3

Viaggio in Scozia

Your Italian friends have just spent 7 days touring Scotland. They are very enthusiastic. Carla sends you the itinerary for their tour. Using this as a basis, try and reconstruct the letter she wrote, giving as many details and being as imaginative as possible:

TOUR PANORAMICO
Lit. 729.000 per pp. inclusa colazione scozzese

I Glasgow/Lomond	1 notte	Loch Lomond
I Fort William	2 notti	Montagne e Coste
I Aviemore	1 notte	Loch Ness & Inverness
I Perthshire	1 notte	Distilleria di Whisky, St. Andrews & Golf, Edimburgo
I Edimburgo/Falkirk	2 notti	Linlithgow, Castello di Edimburgo, Palazzo di Holyrood, Royal Mile, shopping in Princes St

Per agosto supplemento Lit. 81.000

---

e.g. Abbiamo fatto una vacanza bellissima in Scozia. Ci siamo fermati prima …

12 | DESCRIBING THE PAST

Learn how to ...

■ Describe how things were in the past ■ Talk about events or actions which happened regularly in the past ■ Talk about events or actions which were in the process of taking place, when an event or incident occurred ■ Talk about events or actions which had already taken place when an action or event occurred ■ Talk about events or actions which were about to take place

Language points

■ Imperfect tense (**imperfetto**) ■ Using imperfect tense with perfect tense ■ Imperfect tense in conditional sentences (replacing past conditional and/or pluperfect subjunctive) ■ Pluperfect tense (**trapassato**) ■ Past anterior (**trapassato remoto**) ■ Imperfect tense of **stare** and gerund, **stare per** ■ Use of imperfect with **da**

Introduction

Look at the different ways in which the *imperfetto* is used:

Il cielo era azzurro, e il sole splendeva. — *The sky was blue, and the sun was shining.*

Quando lavoravo a Londra prendevo la metropolitana. — *When I worked in London, I took the tube.*

Camminava lungo la strada quando ha visto una cosa stranissima. — *He was walking along the street when he saw something very odd.*

And here is an example of how the *trapassato* (pluperfect) is used:

Eravamo appena entrati quando ha suonato il telefono. — *We had just come in when the telephone rang.*

Focus on grammar

1 Imperfect (imperfetto): *the forms*

The imperfect is formed by adding a set of imperfect endings to the stem of the verb. There are few verbs which have irregular forms in the imperfect.

Verbs ending in *-are*

Mangiare	
mangi**avo**	mangi**avamo**
mangi**avi**	mangi**avate**
mangi**ava**	mangi**avano**

Verbs ending in *-ere*

Leggere	
legge**vo**	legge**vamo**
legge**vi**	legge**vate**
legge**va**	legge**vano**

Verbs ending in *-ire*

Finire	
fin**ivo**	fin**ivamo**
fin**ivi**	fin**ivate**
fin**iva**	fin**ivano**

Slightly unexpected forms include those of verbs with contracted forms of infinitive, such as **bere (bevevo), condurre (conducevo), fare (facevo)**. They derive from the original longer form of these verbs. The pattern is still as above.

2 Imperfect: when to use

a) State, condition, description

When talking about the past, the *passato prossimo* (perfect tense) is used to talk about an action or an event, while the *imperfetto* (imperfect tense) is used to describe a state or condition:

Nell'Ottocento le case **erano** grandi e difficili da pulire ma tutti **avevano** la cameriera.	*In the 19th century, the houses were big and difficult to clean but everyone had maids.*
Ieri **faceva** molto caldo e non **avevo** voglia di mangiare.	*Yesterday it was very hot and I didn't feel like eating.*
La ragazza **era** alta, bionda e **aveva** gli occhi azzurri; **sembrava** svedese.	*The girl was tall, blonde, and had blue eyes; she looked Swedish.*

b) Regular event or action in past

We can also use the *imperfetto* to talk about an action that occurred regularly in the past:

Quando **ero** bambina, **abitavo** a Milano. **Frequentavo** una scuola vicino a casa mia e **andavo** a scuola a piedi.	*When I was a child I lived in Milan. I attended a school near my house and I went to school on foot.*
Quando i miei amici **erano** a Firenze, **pranzavano** in una piccola trattoria e tutti i giorni **mangiavano** lo stesso piatto.	*When my friends were in Florence they had lunch in a little restaurant and every day they ate the same dish.*

c) Incomplete event or action

Lastly the *imperfetto* is used to talk about an action which was never completed (in other words 'imperfect'), often because something else happened to get in the way. The 'something else' is usually expressed with the *passato prossimo*:

Camminavo lungo la strada quando mi **è caduto** un mattone in testa.	*I was walking down the road when a brick fell on my head.*
Parlavamo con i nostri amici quando **è arrivato** un vigile che ci **ha fatto** la multa perché **c'era** divieto di sosta.	*We were talking to our friends when along came a traffic warden who fined us because it was a 'no parking' area.*

It is of course also possible to have two actions occurring simultaneously over a length of time *('I was eating supper as I watched television');* in this case we would use two verbs in the *imperfetto*. Neither action is complete, since they are both described from the point of view of someone watching them at the time.

Guardavo la televisione e   *I was watching the television*
    mangiavo le patatine.   *and eating crisps.*
Mentre **preparava** la cena,   *While she was cooking dinner,*
    cantava.   *she was singing.*

d) Comparison with English

It is not always clear from English usage which is the correct tense to use in Italian; an English verb in the past such as *I went* can be translated in two different ways. Look at these two examples:

Quando ero piccola, **andavo** a   *When I was little, I went to*
    scuola tutti i giorni. *(Imperfetto)*   *school every day.*

Ieri **sono andata** al cinema.   *Yesterday I went to the cinema.*
    (Passato prossimo)

3 Pluperfect (trapassato prossimo): *the forms*

The pluperfect tense *(English: I had eaten, you had eaten,* etc.) is formed by combining the imperfect of the verb **avere** (**avevo**, etc) and the past participle of the appropriate verb:

avevo mangiato	**avevamo** mangiato
avevi mangiato	**avevate** mangiato
aveva mangiato	**avevano** mangiato

In the case of the verbs that use **essere** (see unit 11) the imperfect tense of **essere** (**ero**, etc.) is used along with the past participle. The past participle then has to agree with the number and gender of the subject:

ero arrivato**/a**	**eravamo** arrivat**i/e**
eri arrivato**/a**	**eravate** arrivat**i/e**
era arrivato**/a**	**erano** arrivat**i/e**

4 Pluperfect: when to use

The pluperfect tense is used to describe an action or event which takes place before another past event or action in the past:

Eravamo appena **arrivati** in Italia   *We had just arrived in Italy*
quando mio marito **si è ammalato**.   *when my husband fell ill.*

It can also be used alone to express an action or event which had or had not already taken place:

Mia moglie non **aveva** mai **visto**   *My wife had never seen Venice.*
Venezia.

The pluperfect is often used with one of the following phrases of time:

appena	*as soon as, no sooner (had...) than, just*	prima	*earlier, before*
		quando	*when*
		dopo che	*after*
mai	*never*	siccome	*since*
non ancora	*not yet*	perché	*because*
già	*already*		

Avevo appena **cominciato** i miei   *I had just begun my course at*
studi all'Università quando   *University when my father died.*
è morto mio padre.

I miei cugini non **avevano** mai   *My cousins had never visited*
visitato Londra.   *London.*

Non **avevamo** ancora **cominciato**   *We had not yet started the meeting*
la riunione quando **è andata**   *when the lights went off.*
via la luce.

Mario **era** già **stato** all'estero   *Mario had already been abroad*
molte volte.   *many times.*

Dopo che tu **eri andata** via,   *After you had left, Carla*
è venuta Carla con il fidanzato.   *came with her boyfriend.*

I bambini **erano** stanchi perché   *The children were tired because*
avevano fatto un viaggio   *they had had a very*
molto lungo.   *long journey.*

4 The past anterior (trapassato remoto)

The past anterior is a tense not often used by beginners. It is formed by combining the past historic of the verb **avere** or **essere** (see unit 11) with the past participle. This tense is similar to the pluperfect except that it is used when the main verb is in the past historic and is therefore much less commonly found in everyday use. It is never found alone in a main clause but is always introduced by the phrases **dopo che, non appena, quando**:

Dopo che **ebbero mangiato,** *After they had eaten, they put*
  misero a letto i bambini. *the children to bed.*

Non appena **furono tornati** a casa *As soon as they had got back home,*
  arrivò un amico da Milano. *a friend arrived from Milan.*

Quando **ebbero finito** di studiare, *When they had finished studying,*
  uscirono. *they went out.*

Language plus

1 Stare and the gerund

In the examples given previously (*imperfetto* and *passato prossimo*), the *imperfetto* can be replaced by **stare** + gerund. Unit 6 showed how **stare** was used to express the idea of continuous action in the present; in the same way **stare** can be used in the imperfect tense **(stavo)** with the gerund **(parlando, mettendo, dormendo)** to express the idea of an ongoing action in the past:

Stavamo guardando il *We were watching the news on*
  telegiornale quando **è andata** *TV when the electricity*
  via l'elettricità. *was cut off.*

Cosa **stavi facendo** lì per terra? *What were you doing there on*
  the ground?

2 Stare and per

Stare can also be used in the *imperfetto* with the preposition **per** to say what we were on the point of doing:

Stavo per uscire quando è arrivato *I was about to go out when the*
  il postino. *postman arrived.*

Stavo proprio per telefonarti.   *I was just about to phone you.*

3 Imperfetto *(imperfect) used in polite request*

There are a few special ways in which the imperfect is used (known as 'idiomatic' because they are very much part of the spoken language). One of these is to make a polite request or to ask for something in a less demanding way:

Voleva, signora?   *Can I help you, signora?*
    (Lit: *What did you want?*)
Volevo vedere qualche maglia.   *I would like to see a few sweaters.*
    (Lit: *I wanted to see a*
    few sweaters)

4 Imperfect used to replace the past conditional

Informally, in spoken Italian, the imperfect can be used to replace the past conditional. (See unit 22 for examples of sentences which normally use the past conditional.)

Potevi telefonarmi.
(**avresti potuto** telefonarmi)   *You could have phoned me.*

Dovevi farmi sapere.
(**avresti dovuto** farmi sapere)   *You should have let me know.*

In some conditional sentences, the imperfect replaces *both* the past conditional and the pluperfect subjunctive:

Era meglio se gli **telefonavi** subito.   *It would have been better if you*
(**sarebbe stato** meglio se tu gli   *had phoned him straightaway.*
avessi telefonato subito)

Se **venivi** a casa mia, ti   *If you had come to my house,*
  portavo in giro.   *I would have showed you round.*
(se tu **fossi venuto** a casa mia, ti **avrei portato** in giro)

5 Imperfect used with *da to express the pluperfect*

As we saw in unit 11, **da** can be used with the present tense to express what one *has* been doing for some time (and is still doing):

Studio l'italiano **da** tre anni.   *I have been studying Italian for*
    three years (and I am still
    studying it).

In the same way it can be used with the *imperfetto* to express what one *had* been doing:

Imparavo l'italiano **da** tre anni quando il direttore mi ha mandato in Italia.
I had been studying Italian for three years when the director sent me to Italy.

Stavamo a Oxford già **da** un anno quando abbiamo comprato questa casa.
We had been at Oxford for a year already when we bought this house.

Quando Silvia è venuta a casa mia, non **fumava da** più di un mese.
When Silvia came to my house, she hadn't smoked for over a month.

Language in action

Exercise 1

Spot the past tenses

Highlight or underline the past tenses used in these two accounts and try to understand the difference between the tenses:

■ Why my mother was angry

Andavo a casa lunedì sera quando ho incontrato Marco. Marco andava al bar e così ho deciso di accompagnarlo e prendere qualcosa anch'io. Mia madre intanto mi aspettava a casa e quando sono tornato a casa con tre ore di ritardo, mi ha fatto la predica.

■ My birthday

Per il mio compleanno, mio marito aveva promesso di portarmi a Parigi. Io non c'ero mai stata. Avevamo già preso i biglietti quando la signora che aveva offerto di prendersi cura dei bambini si è ammalata e così abbiamo dovuto portare anche i bambini. È stata una gita poco romantica!

Exercise 2

Having carried out Exercise 1, you should be able to decide for yourself which tense to use in this next passage, where infinitives have been left for you to fill in the correct forms:

(Conoscere) Gianni da solo 5 mesi quando *(decidere)* che *(volere)* sposarci. Quandi *(dare)* la notizia alle nostre famiglie, tutti *(rimanere)* molto sorpresi. *(Ricevere)* tanti consigli e tante prediche. Perché *(sposarsi)* così presto? Perché non *(volere)* aspettare? Chi *(potere)* immaginare che il matrimonio *(potere)* provocare tante discussioni! Mio fratello *(sposarsi)* un anno prima senza tutte queste storie. Ma la situazione *(essere)* diversa, in quanto lui *(conoscere)* la sua futura moglie da 10 anni. *(Essere)* studenti insieme al liceo. Alla fine *(prendere)* la decisione di fidanzarci ma di fissare la data del matrimonio per il 2000. Così tutti i nostri parenti *(avere)* tempo di abituarsi all'idea e di organizzare una bella festa.

13 | TALKING ABOUT THE FUTURE

Learn how to ...

■ Talk about future plans ■ Express probability ■ Express or ask about intention(s)

Language points

■ Future tense (**futuro**) ■ Present tense with future meaning
■ Future perfect ■ Future to express probability ■ Future perfect to express probability ■ Phrases of future time

Introduction

Look at these examples of statements referring to future actions or events:

Domani andrò al mercato.	*Tomorrow I'll go to the market.*
L'anno prossimo andrà a Roma.	*Next year he'll go to Rome.*
Stasera andiamo al cinema.	*Tonight we're going to the cinema.*
Fra un anno avrete finito di studiare.	*In a year, you will have finished studying.*
Marco e Carla saranno già a casa.	*Marco and Carla will be home already.*

Focus on grammar

1 Expressing the future: future or present tense

As in English the future is used to talk about what you are going to do that evening, tomorrow or in the more distant future. As in English, it is often replaced by the present tense:

Domani **andrò** a visitare il Museo.	*Tomorrow I'll go and visit the Museum.*
Domani **vado** a visitare il Museo.	*Tomorrow I'm going to visit the Museum.*
La settimana prossima **andremo** negli Stati Uniti.	*Next week we will go to the USA.*
La settimana prossima **andiamo** negli Stati Uniti.	*Next week we're going to the USA.*

Sometimes the future tense contains the idea of a promise:

| Te lo **porterò** domani. | *I'll bring you it tomorrow.* |
| Ti **telefonerò** la settimana prossima. | *I'll call you next week.* |

2 Forms of the future tense

The future tense is formed by taking the infinitive of the verb (e.g. **parlare**), removing the ending **-are, -ere** or **-ire** and adding the future endings. Here are all the forms of the future tense:

Verbs ending in *-are*

parl**erò**	parl**eremo**
parl**erai**	parl**erete**
parl**erà**	parl**eranno**

Verbs ending in *-ere*

legg**erò**	legg**eremo**
legg**erai**	legg**erete**
legg**erà**	legg**eranno**

Verbs ending in *-ire*

part**irò**	part**iremo**
part**irai**	part**irete**
part**irà**	part**iranno**

Verbs whose future tense is irregular

a) verbs in which the **-e-** of the future is dropped: **andare (andrò);
avere (avrò); cadere (cadrò); dovere (dovrò); potere (potrò);
sapere (saprò); vedere (vedrò); vivere (vivrò).**

b) verbs in which the **-e-** or **-i-** is dropped but which then undergo a
further change: **rimanere (rimarrò); tenere (terrò); valere (varrò);
venire (verrò); volere (vorrò).**

c) those with an already contracted (shortened) infinitive such as **bere**
(to drink) whose future tense has a double **rr** like the verbs listed
above **(berrò).**

d) verbs whose last syllable begins with **-care, -ciare, -gare** or **-giare.**
These undergo spelling changes in order to keep the same sound:

Dropping the 'i': **cominciare (comincerò); lasciare (lascerò);
mangiare (mangerò).** Adding 'h' to keep the sound hard: **cercare
(cercherò); pagare (pagherò).**

e) the one-syllable verbs **dare, dire, fare, stare** which keep the same
verb stem, giving **darò, dirò, farò, starò.**

f) **essere** – future **sarò.**

3 Future tense expressing probability

Often in English you say *He'll be in London by now* using a future form
to express the present with the meaning of probability. The future in
Italian is often used in the same way:

Sarà a Londra.	*He must be in London.*
Sarai stanca.	*You must be tired.*
Avrete fame.	*You must be hungry.*

4 Future perfect

The future perfect (future in the past) is used when you talk about the
future but referring to what you *will have done* by then rather than what
you *will do.*

Per martedì **avrà finito** il libro.   *He will have finished the book
by Tuesday.*

La settimana prossima **sarà** **tornata** in Italia.	*She will have gone back to Italy by next week.*
Saremo morti di fame.	*We will have died from starvation.*

5 Future perfect expressing probability

Like the future, this tense can be used to express probability (what people must have done by the moment in time at which we are speaking):

Gli **sarà successo** qualcosa.	*Something must have happened to him.*
Avrà lasciato il numero di telefono, spero.	*She'll have left her phone number, I hope.*
Avrai già **fatto** le valigie, immagino?	*You must have packed already, I imagine.*

6 Future after quando and se

In English the future tense is not used after *when* or *if*. In Italian either the future or the future perfect should be used after **quando** and **se,** when there is a future verb in the main part of the sentence:

Quando **arriveremo** al mare, i bambini **vorranno** fare subito un bagno.	*When we arrive at the seaside, the children will want to have a swim straightaway.*
Se lo **vedrò,** gli **dirò** qualcosa.	*If I see him, I'll say something to him.*
Quando **arriverete** a Napoli, **dovrete** cercare un albergo.	*When you arrive in Naples, you will have to look for a hotel.*
Quando **avrò trovato** la lettera, te la **farò** vedere.	*When I have found the letter, I'll show it to you it.*

In the last example, the future perfect **avrò trovato** can be replaced by the future or even the present (as can the main verb):

Future:	Quando **troverò** la lettera, te la **farò** vedere.
Present:	Quando **trovo** la lettera, te la **faccio** vedere.

Language Plus

1 Phrases of time

Here are some of the most common phrases of time used with the future:

fra poco	*soon, in a short time*	la settimana prossima	*next week*
fra alcuni giorni	*in a few days*	stasera	*this evening*
fra qualche giorno	*in a few days*	domani	*tomorrow*
fra un mese	*in a month*	dopodomani	*the day after tomorrow*
l'anno prossimo	*next year*		
il mese prossimo	*next month*	allora	*then, at that time*

2 Intention

To say what you intend doing in the future, you can also use:

aver intenzione di	*to intend (doing)*
pensare di	*to think of (doing)*
L'anno prossimo **penso di** lavorare in Italia.	*Next year I think I might work in Italy.*
L'estate prossima **ho intenzione di** venire a trovarti.	*Next summer I intend coming to see you.* (Lit: *to find you,* even if one knows where the person is!)

3 Translating the English 'going to'

English – along with other languages – frequently uses the verb *to go* to express the future as in the sentence *He's going to get his degree next year.* In Italian you cannot use the verb **andare** (*to go*) in this sense. **Andare** only expresses the idea of physically going to a place to do something. The future tense must be used instead.

Language in action

Exercise 1

Conversation between final year students

Write an account of this year's finalists and their intentions. The account should be in the third person and based on the information contained in the conversation.

e.g. Sandra **andrà** in Spagna a lavorare, se ...

Luca	Cosa **farai** l'anno prossimo, quando **sarai laureata**?
Sandra	Penso di andare a lavorare all'estero. Se non trovo un posto qui, **andrò** in Spagna. E tu?
Luca	Mio padre ha un'impresa a Milano. Forse **andrò** a lavorare con lui. Mi **pagherà** bene, e non **dovrò** lavorare troppo.
Sandra	**Vedrai** che fra dieci anni **avrai** già **fatto** i primi miliardi!
Luca	E tu fra dieci anni **avrai** già **sposato** uno spagnolo e **avrai fatto** tre figli!

Exercise 2

Next year's holidays

Translate this conversation between Luisa and Amelia into English.

Luisa	Dove **farete** le vacanze l'anno prossimo?
Amelia	Abbiamo intenzione di andare negli USA. Forse **andremo** a trovare qualche parente. Mio marito non vuole andare in Italia come abbiamo fatto quest'anno.
Luisa	**Sarete** stufi di andare in Italia ormai, e sempre in Calabria. **Avrete visto** tutta la Calabria, no?
Amelia	Beh, tutta no, ma forse **basterà** per adesso!

Exercise 3

Match these halves to make up whole sentences. And then complete them with the correct verb form as appropriate, either present, future or future perfect (the infinitive is supplied in brackets).

First half

1   Quando io *(venire)* a cena …
2   Se tu *(vedere)* Marco …
3   Appena i bambini *(arrivare)* al mare …
4   Quando *(fare)* caldo ….
5   Domani sera quando *(finire)* di lavorare …
6   Ad agosto quando io e mio marito *(andare)* in Argentina …

Second half

A   … il figlio più piccolo *(rimanere)* qui.
B   … i miei zii *(venire)* qui al mare.
C   … gli ospiti *(avere)* sete e *(bisognare)* prendere delle bottiglie di acqua minerale.
D   … *(fare)* un bagno.
E   … digli che lo *(chiamare)* fra alcuni giorni.
F   … vi *(portare)* un regalo.

14 | TALKING ABOUT WANTS AND PREFERENCES

Learn how to ...

■ Express a wish or desire for something ■ Express a wish or desire to do something ■ Express a wish for someone else to do something ■ Express a preference

Language points

■ Present tense of **voglio** to express an immediate want ■ **Volere** used with object or person **(voglio un gelato)** ■ **Volere** used with infinitive **(voglio andare)** ■ Direct object pronouns **lo, la, li, le** ■ Pronoun **ne** ■ Other verbs and infinitive combinations: using **a, di** ■ **preferire** ■ Present conditional **vorrei** to express a wish ■ Idiomatic expressions using **volere (voler bene, ci vuole)**

Introduction

Study these examples of statements expressing a wish, desire or preference, either for yourself or for other people:

Vuole dei soldi.	*He wants some money.*
Li **vuole** subito.	*He wants them straightaway.*
Vuole che io gli presti dei soldi.	*He wants me to lend him money.*
Vorrei una bistecca con insalata verde.	*I would like a steak with green salad.*
Vorremmo vedere il film di Fellini.	*We would like to see the film by Fellini.*
Preferisce viaggiare in aereo.	*She prefers travelling by plane.*
Preferisco che i ragazzi giochino fuori.	*I prefer the kids to play outside.*

Focus on grammar

1 Voglio *(etc.) and direct object pronouns*

Volere *(to want)* is an irregular verb: it does not really follow the pattern of the **-ere** verbs (see unit 5). The forms of the present tense are as follows:

voglio	**vogliamo**
vuoi	**volete**
vuole	**vogliono**

Volere can be used with an object or a person:

Voglio un panino con salame.	*I want a roll with salami.*
Vuole la mamma.	*He wants his mummy.*

Instead of repeating the name of the object wanted, **volere** can be used with direct object pronouns **lo, la, li, le** *(it/them)* to say *I want it* or *I prefer it*, etc. (Unit 4 showed these pronouns used with **ecco**.) They normally go *before* the verb but there are exceptions to this rule (see Grammar appendix). Whether we use **lo** or **la**, **li** or **le** depends on whether the object in question is masculine or feminine, singular or plural:

Non vuoi il caffè, Sandra?	*Don't you want coffee, Sandra?*
No, non **lo** voglio, grazie.	*No. I don't want it, thanks.*
Vuoi la marmellata?	*Do you want jam?*
Sì, **la** voglio.	*Yes, I want it.*
Volete i fagiolini?	*Do you want green beans?*
No, non **li** vogliamo.	*No, we don't want them.*
Volete le patatine?	*Do you want crisps?*
Sì, **le** vogliamo.	*Yes, we want them.*

2 Pronoun ne

When the original question has **dei, delle,** etc. *(some)* or **un, uno, una** with the noun, the correct pronoun to replace it in the answer is **ne** which means *of it, of them*, etc.

Vuole delle melanzane, signora?	*Would you like some aubergines, signora?*
Sì, **ne** vorrei un chilo.	*Yes, I would like a kilo (of them).*

Vuoi un biscotto?	*Do you want a biscuit?*
Sì, **ne** vorrei due.	*Yes, I would like two (of them).*

3 Direct object pronouns with other verbs

All these pronouns can, of course, be used not just with **volere** but with any verb that takes a direct object:

Hai scritto le cartoline?	*Have you written the postcards?*
No, **le** scriverò stasera.	*No, I'll write them tonight.*
Hai visto Luciano al convegno?	*Have you seen Luciano at the conference?*
No, spero di veder**lo** stasera.	*No, I hope to see him tonight.*

When the pronouns come before a *passato prossimo*, the past participle changes its ending according to whether the pronoun is masculine/feminine, singular/plural. More examples can be found in the Grammar Appendix (4.3).

Hai mangiato la pasta con i tartufi?	*Have you eaten pasta with truffles?*
No, non **l'**ho mai mangia**ta**.	*No, I've never eaten it.*

4 Voglio (etc.) and the infinitive

Voglio can be combined with a verb infinitive to say what one wants to do:

Voglio diventare ricca e famosa.	*I want to become rich and famous.*

Desiderare, preferire can also be used in this way:

Desidero iscrivermi al corso.	*I want to enrol for the course.*
Preferisco mangiare presto.	*I prefer to eat early.*

5 Vorrei (etc.) with noun object or verb infinitive

A less abrupt way of saying or asking what one wants is to use the conditional **vorrei** (etc.), the forms of which are given in unit 20:

Vorremmo una camera matrimoniale con bagno.	*We would like a double room with bath.*
Desidererebbero qualcosa da bere?	*Would you like something to drink?*

Vorrei parlare con il direttore, per favore. *I would like to speak to the manager, please.*

Vorrebbe vedere qualche modello, signora? *Would you like to see a few styles, signora?*

6 Other verbs that can be used before the infinitive

Apart from **volere,** many other verbs combine with an infinitive. Sometimes these are joined by the preposition **a,** sometimes they are joined by **di** and sometimes they need no preposition at all. Here are some examples:

a) No preposition required

Verbs include **desiderare** *(to want to)*; **osare** *(to dare)*; **potere** *(to be able to)*; **preferire** *(to prefer)*; **sapere** *(to know)*; **volere** *(to want to)*:

Preferisco prendere il treno. *I prefer to take the train.*
Posso venire con voi? *May I come with you?*
Non **oso** chiedergli niente. *I don't dare ask him anything.*

b) Verbs requiring *a*

These include verbs of beginning, learning, setting out, such as **cominciare** *(to begin)*; **decidersi** *(to resolve to)*; **imparare** *(to learn)*; **iniziare** *(to begin)*; **mettersi** *(to set out to)*:

Comincio a capire. *I begin to understand.*
Imparo a fare windsurf. *I'm learning to windsurf.*

c) Verbs requiring *di*

These include verbs of ending, giving up, such as **finire** *(to end)*; **smettere** *(to stop)*:

Smetto di fumare. *I stop smoking.*
Finisco di lavorare alle cinque. *I stop working at 5 p.m.*

A more complete list of verbs and the prepositions that follow them is found in the Grammar appendix.

Note: In English, the second verb can also be expressed in the gerund or **-ing** form. (The gerund is fully explained in unit 6.) This is not generally possible in Italian, where the infinitive is used, as in the examples shown above (*I stop smoking*: **smetto di fumare**).

d) Verb followed by *che* and the subjunctive

When there are two different people involved, for example when you are ordering or wanting someone else to do something *(I want him to come),* you cannot use the verb and infinitive combination, but have to use **volere** with **che** and a verb form known as the subjunctive:

Voglio che Franco **venga**.	*I want Franco to come.*
Vuole che io **paghi**.	*He wants me to pay.*

For a fuller explanation of this construction, and the full range of tenses, see unit 20.

7 Preferire

Preferire *(to prefer)* can be used with an object or person:

Chi preferisci dei due?	*Who do you prefer of the two?*
Preferisco Nino.	*I prefer Nino.*
Preferisci la birra o il vino?	*Do you prefer beer or wine?*
Preferisco il vino.	*I prefer wine.*

When **preferire** is used to compare two different objects or persons, the English *to* is translated by **a**:

Preferisco il caffè **al** tè.	*I prefer coffee to tea.*
Preferisco Londra **a** Roma.	*I prefer London to Rome.*

Like **volere** or **desiderare**, the verb **preferire** can be used with a direct object or direct object pronoun:

Come **lo** preferisci?	*How do you prefer it?*
Lo preferisco con latte.	*I prefer it with milk.*

Preferire can also be used with a verb:

Preferisci andare al cinema o pattinare?	*Do you prefer going to the cinema or ice skating?*
Preferisco pattinare.	*I prefer skating.*

Language plus

1 Volere

Volere in the perfect tense *(passato prossimo)* normally takes **avere**; but if the verb that follows it is a verb that takes **essere** in the perfect tense (**andare, stare,** etc.) then **volere** can also form the passato prossimo with **essere** (**avere** is equally acceptable nowadays).

Ho voluto vedere la mostra. *I wanted to see the exhibition.*

Sono voluto andare a letto presto. *I wanted to go to bed early.*
(**Ho voluto** andare a letto presto.)

2 Ci vuole

Ci vuole is a phrase that means *it takes* (referring to time); for more than one hour, use the plural form **ci vogliono**:

Da Londra a Oxford **ci vuole** un'ora.	*From London to Oxford it takes one hour.*
Da Londra a Edimburgo **ci vogliono** sei ore in treno.	*From London to Edinburgh it takes 6 hours by train.*

This verb uses **essere** with the passato prossimo:

Da Roma a Reggio Calabria **ci sono volute** sette ore.	*From Rome to Reggio Calabria it took seven hours.*

3 Voler bene a

Voler bene a is an expression meaning *to love*; **bene** is an adverb and does not change:

A chi **vuoi bene**?	*Who do you love?*
Voglio bene al mio cane.	*I love my dog.*

4 *Tenses and moods of* volere

Indicative: imperfect, *passato prossimo*

There tends to be a difference of meaning between these two tenses: **volevo** means *I wanted to* (but I couldn't) and **ho voluto** means *I wanted to* (and I did):

Volevo andare in banca, ma era chiusa.	*I wanted to go to the bank but it was shut.*
Ho voluto andare in banca per cambiare soldi.	*I wanted to go to the bank to change money. (and I did)*

Conditional: present, past

While the present conditional **vorrei** means *I would like,* the past conditional **avrei voluto** means *I would have liked.* There are two different ways of translating the same sentence in English:

> **Avrei voluto** vedere quel film.   *I would have liked to see that film./*
> *I would like to have seen that film.*

Language in action

Exercise 1

Which form of **volere** is more appropriate here? Present or conditional? You choose.

 1 *(Alla banca)*   Scusi, *(volere)* aprire un conto studenti.
 2 *(A casa)*   Sandro, *(volere)* venire con me in centro?
 3 *(A scuola)*   Professore, *(volere)* chiederLe un consiglio.
 4 *(Al bar)*   Ragazzi, *(volere)* andare a mangiare la pizza?
 5 *(In autobus)*   Signora, *(volere)* sedersi?
 6 *(In un negozio)* Signora, scusi, *(volere)* vedere quel maglione.
 7 *(Fuori)*   Ragazzi, *(volere)* venire a casa mia stasera?
 8 *(A casa)*   Mamma, *(volere)* telefonare a Chiara. Mi passi il telefono?
 9 *(A scuola)*   Professore, possiamo finire in anticipo? *(Volere)* andare a casa a guardare la partita.
10 *(Al mare)*   Vada via, La prego. Non *(volere)* né orologi né cinture! Non compriamo niente.

Exercise 2

Convivere è duro

Sara is telling her friends how unfairly her mother treats her. To make it more interesting for you, we have left out **volere** every time it occurs. Use the correct form (tense, mood) of **volere** to fill in the gaps and reproduce what Sara said:

Mia madre è molto difficile. Io ho 15 anni ma mi tratta come una bambina di 12 anni. Non .... che io esca la sera con i miei amici, oppure mi fa uscire ma .... che torni prima di mezzanotte. Io invece .... andare in discoteca con gli altri e rimanere fino alle 2.00. L'altro giorno .... andare al cinema e ho chiesto dei soldi a mia madre, ma lei non .... che io andassi al cinema da sola. Non .... darmi i soldi. .... che io rimanessi sempre a casa con lei.

15 | DESCRIBING PROCESSES AND PROCEDURES

Learn how to ...

■ Say how something is done ■ Say how something ought to be done
■ Give instructions in impersonal form ■ Describe your reactions to
something

Language points

■ Passive using **essere** and past participle **(è fatto)** ■ Passive using
venire (viene fatto) ■ passive using **andare (va fatto)** ■ Passive
using **si passivante** ■ Impersonal **si** ■ **rimanere** and participles

Introduction

Study these examples of passive constructions and their meanings:

La cena è servita.	*Dinner is served.*
La cena viene servita alle 8.00.	*Dinner is served at 8 o'clock.*
La cena va servita alle 8.00.	*Dinner should be served at 8 o'clock.*
Si serve la cena alle 8.00.	*Dinner is served (one serves dinner) at 8 o'clock.*

Focus on grammar

1 Active and passive verbs

In a normal sentence the subject of the sentence is the person or thing
carrying out the action. The verb is therefore called an active verb.
Sometimes the person or thing that is the subject of the sentence is not the

'doer' but is having something 'done' to him/it.   The verb is then described as passive.

2 Passive with essere

To form the passive, use the verb **essere** *(to be)* and the past participle e.g. **parlato, bevuto, capito** *(eaten, drunk, understood)*. The endings of the past participle change according to whether the subject – the person or thing having the action done to them – is masculine or feminine, singular or plural. (See unit 11 for the forms of the past participle.) Here are some examples of passive sentences with **essere**:

I vestiti Benetton **sono** **venduti** in tutta Italia.	*Benetton clothes are sold throughout Italy.*
La bistecca **è cotta** ai ferri.	*The steak is cooked on the grill.*

3 Passive with venire

When the action is carried out regularly, **venire** is often used instead of **essere**:

In Italia gli spaghetti **vengono** **mangiati** spesso.	*In Italy spaghetti are eaten often.*
Il vino **viene bevuto** a tutti i pasti.	*Wine is drunk at all meals.*

4 Passive with andare

When something ought to be done, or must be done, **andare** is used in place of **essere**:

Gli spaghetti **vanno cotti** al dente.	*Spaghetti should be cooked 'al dente'.*
Il vino bianco **va servito** fresco.	*White wine should be served chilled.*

5 Si passivante

Lastly we can make the verb passive by adding the *si passivante* (literally the **si** that makes the verb passive!) to the 3rd person singular or plural *(he, she, they* form) of the verb.

If the person or object which is having the action done to it (or *him, her* or *them)* is singular, the verb will be singular:

In Inghilterra **si legge** il Times anche di sabato.	*In England one reads the Times on Saturdays too.*

A Milano **si mangia** spesso il risotto alla milanese.	*In Milan one often eats risotto milanese.*

If there is more than one person or object involved, the verb must be plural:

In Inghilterra **si leggono** molti libri in lingua straniera.	*In England one reads lots of books in a foreign language.* *(Lit: lots of books are read.)*
D'estate **si noleggiano** le mountain bike.	*In summer mountain bikes are rented out.*

6 Passive: range of tenses

The passive verb construction has the same range of tenses and moods as active verbs:

Imperfetto

In quei giorni il burro **veniva fatto** in casa.	*In those days butter was made at home.*

Futuro

L'uva non **verrà raccolta** prima di ottobre.	*The grapes will not be picked until October.*

Condizionale

Questo vino **andrebbe servito** fresco.	*This wine should be served chilled.*

Passato prossimo

Non **è stato fatto** niente.	*Nothing has been done.*

Trapassato

La camera non **era stata** ancora **preparata**.	*The room had not yet been prepared.*

The past participle changes according to whether the subject is masculine/feminine, singular/plural. In the case of the complex tenses – the last two examples shown above – the past participle of **essere (stato)** must change as well.

Language plus

1 Si passivante *and impersonal* si

A **si** construction such as **si fa,** as well as meaning *it is done,* can also be impersonal and express the English *one,* i.e. **si fa** *(one does).* This construction is referred to as the *si impersonale.*

The *si passivante* (**si** which turns the verb into a passive) is similar in use and meaning to the impersonal **si** *(one)* but with some distinctions, shown below.

The impersonal **si,** used to express *one,* is used only with a singular verb:

In Italia **si pranza** all'una.	*In Italy one dines at 1 p.m.*
Non **si sa** mai.	*One never knows.*

The impersonal **si** construction is unusual in that, although using a singular verb, it always uses a plural adjective or participle:

La sera **si è** sempre **stanchi.**	*In the evening one is always tired.*

The *si passivante,* used to express the passive, can be used with singular or plural:

Si noleggiano biciclette.	*There are bikes for hire.*
Si affitta una casa in centro.	*There is a house for rent in the centre.*

2 Si passivante *used to give instructions*

The **si** construction can be used to explain to someone how to do something, in which case it is translatable in English as *one:*

Prima **si taglia** la cipolla, **si mette** nel tegame, poi **si aggiungono** i pomodori tagliati a pezzetti e **si lasciano** cuocere per mezz'ora.	*First one cuts the onion, one puts it in the pan, then one adds the tomatoes cut into small pieces, and one leaves them to cook for half an hour.*

3 Ci si

When the impersonal **si** *(one)* meets the reflexive pronoun **si** *(himself, herself, itself)* there are problems! In theory, if you want to say *one gets up,* you combine **si** *(one)* with **si** *(himself)* as in **si** alza *(he gets up)* to produce **si si** alza. But to avoid this repetition of **si**, one says **ci si** alza. Here are some other examples:

Ci si veste.	*One gets dressed.*
Ci si vede alle 5.00.	*We meet at 5.00.*
	(Lit: *one sees one another*).

4 Rimanere

To express emotion, the verb **rimanere** (lit: *to remain*) is used with the past participle or an adjective:

Sono rimasto sorpreso.	*I was surprised.*
Mia sorella **è rimasta** delusa.	*My sister was disappointed.*
La casa **è rimasta** distrutta.	*The house was destroyed.*

Other examples of adjectives or participles used with **rimanere** include **offeso** *(hurt, offended)*; **contento** *(happy)*; **scandalizzato** *(shocked)*.

The adverb **male** is also used with **rimanere**:

Siamo rimasti molto **male**.	*We were very hurt.* (not literally)

Italians occasionally use **scioccato** (an English borrowing) for '*shocked*'.

5 Indirect objects

Turning active sentences into passive is not always possible in Italian.

Take these English examples:

He gives the book. →	***He is given** the book.*
	(The book is given to him)
She sends the flowers. →	***She is sent** the flowers.*
	(The flowers are sent to her)

It is not possible to translate the first of each pair of examples literally into Italian. The person being given the book (or the flowers) is an indirect object (one gives something *to* someone) and cannot be used in Italian as the subject of the sentence. Only direct objects can be turned into the subject of a passive sentence in Italian.

This is what happens if we take the examples above and try to turn them into the passive:

He gives the book.	(Lui) dà il libro.
He is given the book.	*Cannot* be translated literally.
The book is given to him.	Il libro gli **viene dato**.
	or Gli **si dà** il libro.
She sends flowers.	(Lei) manda i fiori.
She is sent flowers.	*Cannot* be translated literally.
Flowers are sent to her.	I fiori le **vengono mandati**.
	or Le **si mandano** i fiori.

Language in action

Exercise 1

Holiday 'musts' in Versilia

Highlight or underline all the passive constructions in this short piece of advice from a fashion correspondent:

Si ascolteranno concerti come quello di Gianni Morandi ... al tramonto si visitano gli studi degli scultori. Il mercoledì si va al mercato dove le più belle tovaglie, lenzuola, piatti e bicchieri attendono solo di essere comprati. Tra i colori preferiti, va incluso il bianco: camicie bianche, scarpe da tennis bianche...ecc. L'unica concessione verrà riservata al kaki coloniale.

Exercise 2

How to serve pasta

Even if you don't know how to cook pasta, you can still fill in the gaps using various forms of the passive, either with **andare, essere** or **venire**:

In Italia *(mangiare)* molta pasta. La pasta *(mangiare)* all'ora di pranzo, soprattutto al centro e al sud del paese. Al nord, invece, *(mangiare)* più spesso il riso e la polenta. La pasta *(servire)* con sugo di pomodoro o di carne. *(Servire)* al dente, e quindi non troppo cotta. A Bologna le tagliatelle *(servire)* spesso con prosciutto e panna mentre in Sicilia gli spaghetti *(servire)* con le melanzane.

16 TALKING ABOUT LIKES AND DISLIKES

Learn how to ...

■ Talk about your likes and dislikes ■ Talk about someone else's likes and dislikes ■ Ask someone about their likes and dislikes ■ Contrast your and someone else's likes and dislikes

Language points

■ **piacere** ■ Unstressed indirect object pronouns **mi, ti, gli**, etc.
■ Stressed object pronouns **(a) me, te, lui**, etc. ■ **anche, neanche**

Introduction

Study these examples of how to express likes and dislikes. In each of the pairs of examples shown, the second version is the more emphatic:

Saying what you like:

Mi piace molto Venezia. /
A me piace molto Venezia.

I like Venice a lot.

Mi piacciono le tagliatelle con
  salmone e panna. /
A me piacciono le tagliatelle
  con salmone e panna.

*I like tagliatelle with salmon
and cream.*

Mi piace viaggiare. /
A me piace viaggiare.

I like travelling.

Asking someone else what they like:

Ti piace quel ragazzo? /
A te piace quel ragazzo?

Do you like that boy?

Le piacciono i cannelloni? /   *Do you like cannelloni?*
A Lei piacciono i cannelloni?

Vi piace studiare la lingua italiana? /   *Do you like studying Italian?*
A voi piace studiare la lingua italiana?

Saying what others like:

A mia figlia piace visitare i musei. *My daughter likes visiting museums.*

Le piace visitare i musei. /   *She likes visiting museums.*
A lei piace visitare i musei.
Non gli piace la pizza. /   *He doesn't like pizza.*
A lui non piace la pizza.

Note: Cannelloni and **spaghetti** are plural, as are **lasagne, tagliatelle, rigatoni, maccheroni** and all other forms of pasta.

Focus on grammar

1 Piacere: *present tense*

To say that you like something in Italian, use **piacere** *(to please)* with the indirect pronouns **mi, ti, gli,** *(to me, to you, to him, etc.)* or their emphatic forms (**a me, a te, a lui,** etc.).

Think of **piacere** as meaning *'something is pleasing to me'*. This *something* can be:

- a verb   mi piace mangiare (*I like eating*)
- singular noun   mi piace la pizza (*I like pizza*)
- plural noun   mi piacciono i gelati (*I like ice-creams*)

The forms of **piacere** *(to be pleasing)* normally used are the 3rd person singular **piace** and the 3rd person plural **piacciono**. **Piacere** is used together with the Italian indirect object pronouns **mi, ti, gli**, etc., referring to the person who likes or dislikes, as shown below:

a) To say that one likes doing something, use **piace** followed by the infinitive of the verb (**-are, -ere, -ire**, etc.):

Mi piace fare delle passeggiate.   *I like going for walks.*

b) To say that one likes a person or object (singular), use **piace**:

Ti piace questa maglia?   *Do you like this sweater?*
(Questa maglia **ti piace**?)

c)   To say that one likes persons or objects (plural), use **piacciono**:

> **Le piacciono** queste scarpe.   *She likes these shoes.*
> (Queste scarpe **le piacciono**).

2 Indirect object pronouns: mi, ti, gli, le, Le, ci, vi, gli

You have already met the direct object pronouns **mi, ti, lo, la,** etc. in unit 4. Luckily four of the indirect object pronouns (**mi, ti, ci, vi**) share the same forms. Indirect object pronouns also normally come in the same position, i.e., immediately before the verb (**mi piace, ti piacciono**), which is why they are sometimes called conjunctive ('joining') pronouns. Here are all the indirect object pronouns:

Singular		**Plural**	
mi	*to me*	**ci**	*to us*
ti	*to you*	**vi**	*to you*
gli	*to him*	**gli**	*to them**
le	*to her*		
Le	*to you* (formal)		

*An alternative form meaning *'to them'* is **loro.** This is less common nowadays, although you may see it in written Italian. Unlike the other pronouns, **loro** comes after the verb:

> Abbiamo mandato **loro** un invito.   *We sent them an invitation.*

These indirect pronouns are used with any verb where English uses the prepositions *to* or *for* and with many other verbs (see Grammar Appendix, 4.1, 4.2).

There are exceptions to the rule that pronouns always come *before* the verb, and these are also explained in the Grammar Appendix (4.3).

3 Piacere: *other tenses*

Piacere has a full range of tenses, for example:

Future:

> Vi **piacerà** molto Firenze.   *You will really like Florence.*

Conditional:

Mi **piacerebbe** andare a sciare.   *I would like to go skiing.*

Imperfect:

Gli **piaceva** tanto la cucina   *He really used to like Italian*
  italiana.   *cooking.*

Passato prossimo:

Le **è piaciuta** la gita al lago?   *Did you like the trip to the lake?*

Note: In the *passato prossimo*, **piacere** uses **essere** and not **avere**.

4 Stressed pronouns: (a) me, (a) te, etc.

a) Stressed or unstressed?

To compare likes and dislikes, you can replace the indirect pronouns shown above with a more emphatic ('stressed') form of indirect object pronoun **me, te, lui,** etc., preceded by preposition **a**. These pronouns are also known as disjunctive ('non-joining') pronouns because they are separate from the verb. The examples below show both forms:

Unstressed: Stressed:
Mi piace il caldo.   **A me** piace il caldo.   *I like the heat.*

b) Forms of stressed object pronouns

Here are all the forms of the stressed object pronouns:

Singular		Plural	
a me	*to me*	**a noi**	*to us*
a te	*to you*	**a voi**	*to you*
a lui	*to him*	**a loro**	*to them*
a lei	*to her*		
a Lei	*to you* (formal)		

c) With *anche* or *neanche*

The stressed pronouns can be used with **anche** (*also*), for example **anche a me, anche a te, anche a lui**:

Anche a me piace la pizza.   *I like pizza too.*

And with **neanche** (*not even, neither*), for example **neanche a me** (*not (to) me either, me neither*), **neanche a te**, **neanche a lui**:

Neanche a lui piacciono i funghi.   *He doesn't like mushrooms either.*
(Neither does he like mushrooms)

If **neanche** comes after the verb, it needs **non** before it:

Non piace **neanche a me** lavare   *I don't like washing dishes either.*
i piatti.

In replying to a question, it is not necessary to repeat the verb:

A me piace il mare. E a te?   *I like the seaside. And you?*
Sì. **Anche a me**.   *Yes. Me too.*

5 *Emphatic pronouns used in other contexts*

These stressed (emphatic) pronouns can be used not only with **a** but with other prepositions, such as **con, da, di, in, per, su**:

Sono uscita **con lui**.   *I went out with him.*
L'ho fatto **per te**.   *I did it for you.*

They can also be used without any preposition, simply as a more emphatic form of direct object pronoun or where contrast is needed:

Vuole **me** non **te**.   *He wants **me** not **you**.*

For further information on pronouns, see the Grammar appendix (4) at the back of the book.

Language plus

1 Gradire

Another way of saying what you like is to use **gradire** *(to like)*:

Gradisci una bibita fresca?   *Would you like a cold drink?*
(**tu** form)
Gradisce una granita di caffè?   *Would you like a coffee granita?*
(**Lei** form)

*****una granita** is a coffee ice made with frozen sweetened coffee.

2 Piacere *(1st and 2nd person forms)*

You can also use the first and second persons (*I, you*) with **piacere** when it tends to have the meaning of *to fancy someone*:

Piaci molto a Giancarlo.   *Giancarlo really likes/fancies you.*
                                          (Lit: *you really please him.*)
Dimmi, ti **piaccio** veramente?   *Tell me, do you really like me?*
                                          (Lit: *do I really please you?*)

3 Volere bene, amare

It is more common to express the idea of liking a person with **volere bene a** *(to love, like a lot)* or **amare** (to love):

Vuoi bene a Michele?   *Do you love Michele?*
Ti vuole bene?   *Does he love you?*
Amo soltanto mio marito.   *I only love my husband.*

Language in action

Exercise 1

Going to the cinema

Fill in the gaps with the correct form of **piacere** or an indirect object pronoun to say what kind of film Anna, Mara and Anna's husband like watching:

Anna   Ti .... andare al cinema?
Mara   Sì, mi .... molto. E a te?
Anna   Sì, anche .... piace.
Mara   Che film ti ....?
Anna   A… .... i film romantici ma a mio marito non .... i film di questo genere.
Mara   E .... che tipi di film ....?
Anna   Nessuno.

Exercise 2

Preferences

What do people like eating? Find out by looking at the illustration below and answer the questions on people's likes:

e.g. Cosa piace a Franco?
Gli piacciono le mele.

1   Cosa piace ai bambini?
2   Cosa piace alla mamma?
3   Cosa piace a voi, ragazze?
4   Cosa piace al Presidente degli USA?
5   Cosa piace alla regina d'Inghilterra?
6   Cosa piace agli studenti?
7   Cosa piace agli argentini?
8   Cosa piace a te? *(whatever you like!)*

17 ASKING AND GIVING AN OPINION

Learn how to ...

■ Express a belief or an opinion ■ Ask someone else's opinion
■ Express a rumour ■ Express a tentative view

Language points

■ Subjunctive mood ■ **sembrare, parere** and **pensare, credere**
■ **pensare**, etc. with **che** and the subjunctive ■ **pensare**, etc. with **di**
and the infinitive ■ Phrases expressing opinions ■ **pensare di**,
offering an opinion ■ **magari**

Introduction

There are many ways of expressing an opinion in Italian. One is to use the
indirect object pronouns **mi, ti, gli** (*to me, to you, to him,* etc.) described
in unit 16, along with the verbs **sembrare** or **parere** (*to seem*). Another
way is to use **pensare** or **credere** (*to think*). With these verbs, you often
need to use a verb form known as the subjunctive, which is explained
below.

Study these examples and their English translation before going on:

Come ti sembra questa proposta?	*What do you think of this proposal?* (Lit: *How does this proposal seem to you?*)
Questo ragazzo non mi sembra molto intelligente.	*This boy doesn't seem very bright to me.*
Mi pare che sia fattibile.	*It seems to me that it is feasible.*
Credo che sia una buona idea.	*I think it is a good idea.*

Luigi pensa che l'albergo sia caro.   *Luigi thinks the hotel is dear.*

Mi sembra di aver già visto   *I think I have seen this*
  questo programma.   *programme already.*

Mi pare di conoscere questo signore. *I think I know this gentleman.*

Penso di essere in ritardo.   *I think I am late.*

Crede di aver sbagliato.   *He thinks he has made a mistake.*

Focus on grammar

1 The subjunctive: an introduction

The subjunctive is a 'mood' of the verb used in certain circumstances. The subjunctive is almost extinct in English but – like the dinosaur – a few remnants of it can be found, for example: *I wish he were here*, in which *were* replaces the usual verb form *was*. In Italian it is far from extinct; in fact it is difficult to express a feeling or opinion, doubt or uncertainty, without using it. Units 17, 18, 19 and 20 illustrate different situations in which the subjunctive is used.

It is rarely found on its own (except for expressing an order, see unit 9), but is almost always used in a subordinate clause, i.e. a clause or part of a sentence which depends on the first or main part of the sentence. Usually the second half of the sentence – normally the subordinate clause – is introduced by **che** or another joining word. Look at these examples and the English translation:

Normal (indicative) form of verb:

  Donatella è simpatica.   *Donatella is nice.*

Subjunctive form of verb:

  Non penso che Donatella **sia**   *I don't think Donatella is nice.*
  simpatica.

Normal (indicative) form of verb:

  Marco è antipatico.   *Marco is unpleasant.*

Subjunctive form of verb:

  Mi pare che Marco **sia** antipatico. *I think Marco is unpleasant.*

2 Subjunctive forms: regular verbs

The forms of the present tense of the subjunctive are as follows:

Verbs ending in -are

parlare	
Che parli	parliamo
parli	parliate
parli	parlino

Verbs ending in -ere

mettere	
Che metta	mettiamo
metta	mettiate
metta	mettano

Verbs ending in -ire

partire	
Che parta	partiamo
parta	partiate
parta	partano

capire	
Che capisca	capiamo
capisca	capiate
capisca	capiscano

The many other uses of the subjunctive are covered in units 18, 19 and 20.

3 Subjunctive forms: irregular verbs

There are several verbs for which the form of the subjunctive is slightly different from what you might expect. These are listed in the verb table at the back of the book. Sometimes the 1st, 2nd, 3rd person singular (**io, tu, lui/lei**) and the 3rd person plural (**loro**) are irregular; while the 1st and 2nd person plural (**noi, voi**) are regular.

The most common are the following:

andare	*(to go)*	che io vada	che noi andiamo
avere	*(to have)*	che io abbia	che noi abbiamo
dare	*(to give)*	che io dia	che noi diamo
dire	*(to say)*	che io dica	che noi diciamo
dovere	*(to have to)*	che io debba	che noi dobbiamo
essere	*(to be)*	che io sia	che noi siamo
fare	*(to do)*	che io faccia	che noi facciamo
potere	*(to be able to)*	che io possa	che noi possiamo
stare	*(to be)*	che io stia	che noi stiamo
venire	*(to come)*	che io venga	che noi veniamo
volere	*(to want to)*	che io voglia	che noi vogliamo

4 Sembrare, parere *used to express an opinion*

To express an opinion, you can use **sembrare** *(to seem)* or **parere** *(to appear)*. These verbs are often used impersonally in the 3rd person forms **sembra, pare** *(it seems, it appears),* together with indirect object pronouns **mi, ti, gli** *(to me, to you, to him,* etc.). **Sembrare** and **parere** when used impersonally *(it seems to me)* can be used in two ways:

a) Followed by *di* and the infinitive:

If the person expressing the opinion is the same person carrying out the action in the other part of the sentence, the two parts can be linked by **di,** and the second verb will be in the infinitive form:

Mi sembra di sognare.	*I think I'm dreaming.*
Gli sembra di sbagliare.	*He thinks he is making a mistake.*

You can also use a past infinitive, formed by combining **avere** or **essere** with the past participle:

> **Mi sembra di** aver già visto questo film.
>
> *I think I've seen this film already.*

> **Mi pare di** essere arrivata troppo tardi.
>
> *I think I have arrived too late.*

Note that the final **e** of **avere** or **essere** is often dropped.

b) Followed by *che* and the subjunctive

If on the other hand there is a different subject in each part of the sentence, the two parts of the sentence must be linked by the conjunction **che** *(that)* followed by a verb in the subjunctive:

> **Mi sembra che** lui **sia** un po' pigro.
>
> *I think (that) **he** is a bit lazy.*

> **Gli sembra che** lei **sia** offesa.
>
> *He thinks (that) **she** is offended.*

In English *that* can be omitted, but in Italian **che** cannot be omitted.

5 Sembrare *used personally*

Sembrare can also be used 'personally' i.e. with a subject other than *it* as in the examples below:

> Come ti sembra **il corso**?
>
> *How does the course seem to you?*

> Mi sembra ben organizzato.
>
> *It (the course) seems well-organised to me.*

> **Gianna** mi sembra stanca.
>
> *Gianna looks tired to me.*

Italian uses **come** *(how)* where English would normally say *'What (is it) like?'*

6 Pensare, credere *used to express an opinion*

You can also express an opinion using the verbs **pensare** or **credere**. Like **sembrare, parere**, they can be followed, when the subject is the same, by a simple **di** and the infinitive; when the subject is different, the two parts of the sentence must be linked with **che** and the second verb must be a subjunctive:

a) Followed by *di* and infinitive

> Penso di sognare.
>
> *I think **I'm** dreaming.*

> Pensa di vincere.
>
> *He thinks **he** will win.*

b) Followed by *che* and subjunctive

Pensa che tu stia sognando.	*He thinks **you're** dreaming.*
Penso che Venezia sia la città più bella del mondo.	*I think **Venice** is the most beautiful city in the world.*

7 *Phrases expressing opinion*

Here are some of the most common phrases of opinion:

a mio parere	*in my opinion*
per me	*in my opinion*
secondo me	*in my opinion*
per quanto mi riguarda	*as far as I am concerned*

These phrases do not need to be followed by **che** and the subjunctive. They are simply added on to the rest of the sentence:

A mio parere è un po' caro.	*In my opinion it's a little dear.*
Per quanto mi riguarda, non vale la pena vederlo.	*As far as I am concerned, it's not worth the trouble of seeing it.*

Language plus

1 *Expressing opinion or rumour (conditional)*

Often when an opinion is expressed or rumour is voiced, Italians use the conditional (see unit 20) to express the present tense:

Secondo la stampa, l'Italia **sarebbe** al quinto posto nella graduatoria dei paesi industrializzati.	*According to the press, Italy is in fifth place in the league table of industrialised nations.*

2 Sembra di sì, sembra di no

Note the following idiomatic expressions:

Mi sembra **di sì**.	*I think so.*
Mi sembra **di no**.	*I think not/I don't think so.*

These can be replaced by the following:

Mi pare di sì. / Penso di sì. / Credo di sì.   *I think so.*
Mi pare di no. / Penso di no. /Credo di no. *I think not/I don't think so.*

3 Using pensare di to express an opinion

To express an opinion about someone or something, use **pensare di** *(to think of)*:

Cosa pensi di questa maglietta?	*What do you think of this t-shirt?*
Cosa **ne** pensi?	*What do you think of it?*
Cosa pensi di questi sandali?	*What do you think of these sandals?*
Cosa **ne** pensi?	*What do you think of them?*

4 Tenses of the subjunctive

The subjunctive is found in a variety of tenses, not only in the present tense illustrated above.

Here are some examples of its other tenses:

Imperfetto

Credevo che **fosse** stanco.   *I thought he was tired.*

Passato prossimo

Credo che **sia arrivato** ieri.   *I think he arrrived yesterday.*

Trapassato

Credevo che **fosse** già **arrivato**.   *I thought he had already arrived.*

The imperfect and the pluperfect subjunctive are described in greater detail in units 20 and 21.

5 How to form the perfect subjunctive

Use the present subjunctive of the verb **avere (abbia,** etc.) or, in the case of verbs taking **essere,** the verb **essere (sia,** etc.) with the past participle of the verb required (e.g. **comprato**) to form the perfect tense of the subjunctive (see also unit 11):

Non credo che lui mi **abbia** **comprato** un regalo.	*I don't think he has bought me a present.*
Non mi pare che lei **sia partita**.	*I don't think she has left.*

6 When to use the perfect subjunctive

The perfect subjunctive should be used anywhere you would use the perfect tense in a 'normal' sentence, i.e. to describe an action which has already taken place. It generally comes in a sentence where the main verb is in either present, future or occasionally perfect:

Non **credo** che il treno **sia** già **partito**.
I don't think the train has left already.

Visiteremo gli scavi a meno che i tombaroli non **abbiano portato** via tutto.
We will visit the excavations unless the grave-robbers have taken everything away.

In general, a perfect tense in the main clause is followed by an imperfect or pluperfect subjunctive:

Non mi **è sembrato** che lui **fosse** particolarmente brillante.

It didn't seem to me that he was particularly brilliant.

7 Magari

Magari is often used when someone is giving an opinion. It usually means *maybe* or *perhaps*:

Magari lui sa dov'è.
Maybe he knows where it is.

Sometimes **magari** means a little bit more. Used at the beginning of a sentence (where it is followed by the imperfect subjunctive), or on its own it can express a hope that something might come about:

Magari avessi la possibilità...
If only I had the chance …

Pensate di comprare una nuova macchina quest'anno?
Are you thinking of buying a new car this year?

Magari!
I wish we were! / I wish we could!

(The meaning implied by **magari** is that it is very unlikely to happen.)

Language in action

Exercise 1

Corso estivo a Oxford

Your friend Cristina wants to send her son Filippo to Oxford to do an English course. She has found a school that might be suitable. Offer her your opinion on the various aspects of the summer school, numbered below, using any of the expressions you have learnt, for example, **pensare, credere, mi sembra, mi pare**.

e.g. È importante scegliere una scuola seria?
Io penso che **sia** molto importante scegliere una scuola seria.

1 Bastano 50 sterline di *pocket money* alla settimana?
2 La scuola è membro dell'ARELS (Association of Recognised English Language Schools)?
3 La scuola sta vicino al centro?
4 La scuola ha insegnanti qualificati?
5 Gli insegnanti hanno esperienza con ragazzi giovani?
6 I ragazzi possono praticare lo sport?
7 I ragazzi devono essere autonomi?
8 La scuola organizza escursioni e attività sociali?
9 I pasti sono tutti inclusi nel prezzo?
10 I ragazzi hanno la possibilità di comprare bibite e merendine?
11 C'è un centro medico nel caso di qualche incidente?

Exercise 2

How wrong can you be?

Your mother thinks you are a saint. Little does she know… Here is a list of the things you really do. Now say what your mother thinks you do!

e.g. Fumo un pacchetto di sigarette al giorno.
Mia madre pensa **che io non abbia mai fumato / che io non fumi**.

1 Vado a letto dopo le due.
Mia madre … *(prima di mezzanotte)*
2 In camera mia leggo riviste e ascolto la musica.
Mia madre … *(studiare)*
3 Ho preso un brutto voto all'esame di storia.
Mia madre … *(prendere un bel voto)*
4 Sono stata bocciata proprio in inglese.
Mia madre … *(essere promossa in tutte le materie)*
5 La sera vado al club.
Mia madre … *(stare a casa della mia amica)*
6 Esco con tanti ragazzi.
Mia madre … *(non uscire con nessuno)*
7 I miei amici sono tutti pazzi.
Mia madre … *(essere ragazzi seri)*
8 Porto sempre la macchina.
Mia madre … *(andare in autobus)*
9 Mangio un chilo di cioccolato al giorno.
Mia madre … *(non mangiare mai cose di quel tipo)*
10 Bevo due bottiglie di vino al giorno.
Mia madre … *(non bere mai alcolici)*

18 EXPRESSING OBLIGATION AND NEED

Learn how to ...

■ Express obligation ■ Ask about someone else's obligations
■ Express one's needs ■ Ask about someone else's needs ■ Express a necessity ■ Say what is needed

Language points

■ **dovere** ■ **aver bisogno di** ■ **bisogna** ■ **c'è bisogno di** ■ **è necessario/essenziale**, etc. ■ **occorre, occorrono, ci vogliono**
■ Using infinitive or **che** and subjunctive, after impersonal verbs

Introduction

The verb **dovere** is used to express obligation (*something we have to do*) and need (*something one needs to do, has to do, must do*). Other ways to express need in Italian include **bisogna, aver bisogno di, c'è bisogno di**.

Study these examples and see if you can spot the differences in meaning between them:

Maria deve studiare di più.	*Maria must study more.* *(Maria needs to study more.)*
Devo andare a casa. È tardi.	*I must go home. It's late.* *(I need to go home. It's late.)*
Ho bisogno di andare in bagno.	*I need to go to the bathroom.*
Bisogna pagare il supplemento.	*One must pay a supplement.*
Non c'è bisogno di pagare il supplemento.	*There's no need to pay the supplement.*

Focus on grammar

1 Dovere

Dovere is a mildly irregular verb which means *(I) must, (I) have to*:

devo	dobbiamo
devi	dovete
deve	devono

Used in the conditional (see unit 20) **dovere** can also mean should, ought to:

Dovrei andare a trovare gli amici inglesi.	*I ought to go and visit my English friends.*
Dovresti visitare la cattedrale.	*You ought to visit the cathedral.*

To talk about the past, either the imperfect tense or the *passato prossimo* can be used, depending on whether the action happened regularly (imperfect) or once only (*passato prossimo*):

Quando ero bambina, **dovevo** andare a scuola a piedi.	*When I was a child, I had to go to school on foot.*
Ieri **ho dovuto** comprare una nuova gomma.	*Yesterday I had to buy a new tyre.*

To say what one should have done, use the past conditional:

Avresti dovuto telefonargli.	*You should have called him.*

2 Aver bisogno di

The phrase **aver bisogno di** (*to have need of*) can be used either with a verb (infinitive form), when talking about an action one has to take, or with a noun, talking about an object or objects one needs; it is normally used personally, referring to a particular person. Obviously, **avere** changes depending on the person referred to, while **bisogno** does not:

Ha bisogno di telefonare.	*She needs to telephone.*
Hanno bisogno di una mano.	*They need a hand.*

3 Bisogna

Bisogna can only be used with a verb (infinitive form) not an object. It is an impersonal verb with a general or impersonal meaning (*one needs, it* *is necessary*), not referring to a particular person. It can be used in two different ways.

a) in a general sense, not referring to a particular person, followed by a verb in the infinitive:

Bisogna pagare alla cassa.   *One must pay at the cash desk.*

b) in a 'personalised' way, mentioning the person or people who are to carry out the action, followed by **che** and the subjunctive (see unit 17):

Bisogna che Lei mi **dica** la data   *You must tell me the departure*
di partenza.   *date.*
                                             (Lit: *It is necessary that you tell*
                                             me the departure date.)

4 C'è bisogno di

In certain situations, **bisogna** can be replaced by a similar 'impersonal' phrase **c'è bisogno** (*there is need of*), which can also be used in two different ways:

a) in a general sense, followed by **di** and the infinitive:

Non c'è bisogno di firmare, vero?   *There's no need to sign, is there?*

b) referring to a particular person or people, using **che** and the subjunctive:

Non c'è bisogno che Lei mi dia   *There isn't any need for you to*
il passaporto.   *give me your passport.*

5 È necessario / essenziale

This impersonal expression can again be used in two ways:

a) as a general statement, followed directly by the infinitive:

È necessario fare il biglietto.   *It is necessary to buy a ticket.*

b) specifying the person or people involved, using **che** and the subjunctive:

È essenziale che tutti i visitatori   *It is essential that all visitors buy*
facciano il biglietto.   *a ticket.*

6 Occorre (it is necessary)

Occorre (*it is necessary*) can be used in the same two ways as the expressions shown above:

a) as a general statement, followed directly by the infinitive:

Occorre prendere il treno.   *It's necessary to take the train.*

b) specifying the person or people involved, followed by **che** and the subjunctive:

Occorre che voi siate pronti per   *You must be ready at 10.00.*
le 10.00.

Note: Any of the expressions listed above can, of course, be replaced simply by using the verb **dovere**, as illustrated in paragraph 1.

7 Occorre, occorrono, ci vogliono

Occorre, occorrono can also be used with an object rather than a verb, meaning *to be needed*. Unlike **aver bisogno di** (see above) **occorre** can be used impersonally, with no particular person mentioned, to make a general statement. If the object needed is singular, the verb must be singular, if plural the verb must be plural:

Per le cartoline **occorre** un   *For postcards one needs a L.750*
francobollo da L.750.   *stamp.*

Per telefonare a Roma, **occorrono**   *To phone Rome, one needs at*
almeno venti monete.   *least twenty coins.*

In this last example **occorre** can be substituted by **ci vogliono** or **servono**:

Per telefonare a Roma, **ci vogliono**   *To phone Rome, one needs at*
almeno venti monete.   *least twenty coins.*

Per telefonare a Roma, **servono**   *To phone Rome, one needs at*
almeno venti monete.   *least twenty coins.*

Occorre can be personalised by adding an indirect object pronoun such as **mi, ti, gli,** etc. or even the name or title of a person:

Mi occorrono cinque francobolli.   *I need five stamps.*
Gli occorre la macchina.   *He needs the car.*
Quante uova **ti occorrono**?   *How many eggs do you need?*
Al direttore **occorrono** le ultime   *The manager needs the latest*
cifre di questo mese.   *figures for this month.*

Language plus

1 More impersonal verbs

There are many other 'impersonal' verbs, i.e. verbs that are used mainly in the third person (*It is necessary*). Some of these can be used with the indirect object pronouns **mi, ti, gli,** etc.(see unit 16) to 'personalise' them. Most of them can be followed either by the infinitive or by **che** and the subjunctive (see unit 17). Examples of such verbs include **basta** (*it is enough to*), **conviene** (*it is best, it is convenient, it is worth*), **pare, sembra** (*it appears, it seems*).

Study these examples:

Basta guardare per capire come ha fatto.	*One only has to look to see how he did it.*
Basta che voi me lo chiediate.	*All you have to do is ask me for it.*
Mi pare di sentire qualcosa.	*I think I can hear something.*
Mi pare che tu non sia convinto.	*It seems to me that you aren't convinced.*
Conviene prendere il treno.	*It's best to take the train.*
Ti conviene prendere il treno.	*It is best for you to take the train.*

2 Impersonal expressions with essere (to be) and adjectives

There are also some impersonal expressions formed by **essere** (*to be*) and various adjectives, such as **è necessario** already mentioned above. Like the impersonal verbs, most of these expressions can be followed by either the infinitive or **che** and the subjunctive. Here are some examples:

È possibile	*It's possible*	**È difficile**	*It's difficult / it's unlikely**
È impossibile	*It's impossible*		
È probabile	*It's probable*	**È utile**	*It's useful*
È improbabile	*It's unlikely*	**È inutile**	*It's useless*
È necessario	*It's necessary*	**È bello**	*It's nice*
È essenziale	*It's essential*	**È bene**	*It's good*
È importante	*It's important*	**È male**	*It's bad*
È facile	*It's easy / it's likely**	**È meglio**	*It's better*

È peggio	*It's worse*	**È naturale**	*It's natural*
È preferibile	*It's preferable*	**È strano**	*It's strange*

È possibile andare in pullman.	*It's possible to go by coach.*
È importante conservare lo scontrino.	*It is important to keep the receipt.*
È facile sbagliare.	*It's easy to make mistakes.*
È bello stare al mare.	*It's nice being at the seaside.*
È strano vedere Roma d'inverno.	*It's strange seeing Rome in winter.*
È peggio andare in campeggio che dormire in un ostello.	*It's worse camping than sleeping in a hostel.*
È possibile che lui sia ancora in Italia.	*It's possible that he is still in Italy.*
È probabile che noi partiamo sabato.	*It's likely that we'll leave on Saturday.*
È naturale che tu abbia voglia di tornare.	*It's natural that you should want to return.*
È strano che loro non abbiano telefonato.	*It's odd that they haven't telephoned.*
È meglio che Lei non torni tardi.	It's better that you don't came back late.

* **È facile** and **È difficile** followed by **che** and the subjunctive often mean *It's likely, it's unlikely* rather than their literal meaning:

È facile che ti scotti se non metti la crema.	*It's likely that you will burn if you don't put cream on.*
È difficile che ci siano ritardi.	*It's unlikely that there will be delays.*

Language in action

Exercise 1

At the railway station

Substitute the phrases in bold with a different phrase expressing need:

Viaggiatore   Un biglietto di andata a ritorno per Roma, per favore. Prima classe.

Impiegato	A che ora vuole partire?
Viaggiatore	**Devo essere** a Roma per le cinque di sera. Che treno **bisogna prendere**?
Impiegato	Se Lei **ha bisogno di** essere a Roma per le 5, **dovrebbe prendere** il treno delle 12.35, che arriva a Roma alle 16.30. È un rapido, però, **bisogna pagare** anche il supplemento.
Viaggiatore	Va bene. Quant'è?
Impiegato	Sono L.39.700 andata e ritorno, compreso il supplemento. **Ha bisogno** di altre informazioni?
Viaggiatore	No, grazie.

Exercise 2

Give some advice to these famous (and less famous) figures. Using one of the expressions explained above, say what you think they should do, either this week, this year or in general:

 1 Il Papa
 2 I bambini
 3 L'insegnante
 4 Tuo marito / tua moglie
 5 Il Presidente della Repubblica
 6 Il Primo Ministro della Gran Bretagna
 7 Il Presidente degli USA
 8 Il tuo vicino di casa
 9 Tua madre / tuo padre
10 Il giornalaio

Exercise 3

Give practical advice to your friends and family:

e.g. Se non vuoi avere freddo …
     Se non vuoi avere freddo, **bisogna che tu metta una maglia**.

1 Ragazzi, se volete giocare a calcio …
2 Se ti piacciono le lasagne …
3 Se hai mal di stomaco …
4 Se sei raffreddato …
5 Se vuoi essere autonomo …

Exercise 4

Agony aunt

You are Irma, the agony aunt on a local newspaper. You receive the letter below. Write a reply to it, saying what the corrrespondent ought to do, and using as many of the expressions you have learned as possible:

Cara Irma

Tra poco nascerà la mia prima bimba e io non so come comportarmi per quanto riguarda gli annunci di nascita. Sui bigliettini si stampa solo il primo nome del bambino o anche eventuali altri nomi? Quando si inviano a parenti e amici? Subito dopo la nascita, oppure in occasione del battesimo, considerando che quest'ultimo potrebbe essere dopo circa due mesi? I confetti quando devono essere offerti? Solo al ricevimento di battesimo o anche prima a chi non vi parteciperà?

(Chiara, Monza)

Cara Chiara,

Ecco alcune regole che ti potranno essere di aiuto. Per gli annunci, non c'è bisogno che voi ...

19 EXPRESSING EMOTIONS AND UNCERTAINTY

Learn how to ...

■ Express emotions or feelings ■ Express doubt and uncertainty ■ Express possibility and probability ■ Express a wish and request for others

Language points

■ Subjunctive after verbs of hoping, fearing, and other emotions
■ Subjunctive after impersonal verbs and other verbs ■ Subjunctive after certain conjunctions ■ Subjunctive used in other situations
■ Deciding whether to use subjunctive or indicative

Introduction

In Italian you need to use the subjunctive whenever something is a possibility, rather than a definite event. It indicates a feeling rather than a reality. For example, it is used with verbs expressing pleasure, hope, fear or sorrow:

Puoi venire stasera?	*Can you come tonight?*
Spero che tu possa venire.	*I hope you can come.*
Michele è in ritardo.	*Michele is late.*
Temo che Michele sia in ritardo.	*I am afraid Michele is late.*
Vi siete divertiti.	*You enjoyed yourselves.*
Sono contenta che vi siate divertiti.	*I am glad that you enjoyed yourselves.*

In each of the examples above, the first statement or question contains the 'normal' (indicative) form of the verb; the second has the subjunctive form, used after **spero** *(I hope)*, **temo** *(I fear)* and **sono contenta** *(I am glad)*.

Focus on grammar

When to use the subjunctive

Some of the verbs or verb phrases that require the subjunctive have been seen already in unit 17 (to express need or necessity) and unit 18 (to express an opinion). Here now are some further examples of how the subjunctive is used. It is most frequently used in the first two situations illustrated, i.e. after certain verbs/verb phrases and after certain conjunctions.

1 After certain verbs or verb phrases

In the examples that follow, while English uses a normal (indicative) verb form, Italian generally uses the subjunctive. A verb in the subjunctive almost always depends on a main verb or verb phrase (the verb found in the main part of the sentence) and is normally introduced by **che**:

a) Emotions or feelings

After any verb or phrase expressing emotion such as **sperare** (*to hope*), **temere** (*to fear*), **piacere, essere contento** (*to be happy*), **essere arrabbiato** (*to be angry*), **essere sorpreso** (*to be surprised*), **vergognarsi** (*to be ashamed*), **mi dispiace** (*to regret, be sorry*), **mi rincresce** (*to regret*), **è un peccato** (*it's a pity*):

Temo che lui **abbia** troppo da fare. *I'm afraid he has too much to do.*

Mi dispiace che tu **sia** impegnata stasera. *I'm sorry that you're busy tonight.*

È un peccato che i bambini non **possano** venire. *It's a pity that the children can't come.*

b) Belief, doubt or uncertainty

After most verbs expressing belief such as **credere, pensare, ritenere** or doubt such as **dubitare**:

Non credo che **costi** troppo. *I don't think it costs too much.*

Dubito che il treno **parta** in orario. *I doubt if the train will leave on time.*

Ritengono che **sia** una persona degna di fiducia. *They maintain that he is a trustworthy person.*

Note, however, that in spoken informal speech, verbs such as **credere**, **pensare**, **ritenere** are often followed by the normal indicative form, either present or future:

Credo che lui **sia** un parente di Amelia. *I think he's a relative*
  (*more formal*)   *of Amelia.*
Credo che lui **è** un parente di Amelia. (*informal*)
Penso che **vanno / andranno** a piedi.   *I think they'll go*
  (*informal*)   *on foot.*

Some verbs, for example **dire**, **sapere**, **vedere**, are followed by the subjunctive *only* when they are negative or when (in the case of **dicono**) they express hearsay:

So che **ha** una macchina.   *I know she has a car.*
Non so se **abbia** una macchina.   *I don't know if she has a car.*

Dico che **è** bravissimo.   *I say he's very clever.*
Dicono che Joan Collins **abbia**   *They say that Joan Collins has*
  fatto vari lifting.   *had several face lifts.*
Non dico che **sia** stupido.   *I'm not saying he's stupid.*

Vedo che tuo marito **è** stanco.   *I see that your husband is tired.*
Non vedo perché tu non **possa**   *I don't see why you can't do it*
  farlo da solo.   *yourself.*

For other examples of **credere, pensare**, see unit 17.

c) Possibility, probability

After verbs and verb phrases expressing possibility, such as **è possibile / impossibile**, **è probabile / improbabile / poco probabile** and **può darsi**:

Può darsi che te lo **riparino** gratis. *Maybe they'll repair it for you*
                                              free of charge.
È impossibile che lui non **abbia**   *It's impossible for him not to have*
  capito.   *understood.*

Similarly, the expressions **è facile / difficile** – as well as the meaning *it is easy / difficult* – can also mean *it is likely / unlikely*:

È facile che gli studenti **sbaglino**.   *It's likely that the students will*
                                              get things wrong.

È difficile che gli studenti   *It's unlikely that the students will*
  capiscano tutto.   *understand everything.*

See unit 18 for a more complete list of impersonal phrases of this type.

d) Wishing, requesting

After verbs such as **volere, chiedere, ordinare,** when one wants someone else to do something:

Voglio che lui **stia** più attento.	*I want him to be more careful.*
Vorrebbe che i bambini **facessero** meno rumore.	*He would like the children to make less noise.*

The conditional form **vorrei** tends to take the imperfect tense of the subjunctive and can be studied in more detail in unit 20.

e) Allowing, forbidding, denying

After verbs such as **permettere** (*to allow*), **vietare** (*to forbid*), **impedire** (*to prevent*) and **negare** (*to deny*):

Non **permette** che i bambini **giochino** in mezzo alla strada.	*She does not allow the children to play in the street.*
Nega che il cane **sia** pericoloso.	*She denies that the dog is dangerous.*

f) Waiting, expecting

After verbs such as **aspettare, aspettarsi** (*to wait for, to expect*):

Mi aspetto che tu **sia** puntuale.	*I expect you to be punctual.*
Aspetto che **arrivino** loro per cominciare.	*I am waiting for them to arrive before starting.*

g) Verbs that introduce an indirect question

In a question introduced by verbs such as **mi chiedo, mi domando** (*I ask, I wonder why*):

Mi chiedo perché lui **sia** così nervoso.	*I wonder why he's so edgy.*

h) Impersonal verbs or expressions ('it' verbs)

The subjunctive is used after impersonal verbs (e.g. **bisogna, conviene**) or phrases composed of **essere** and adjective (**è necessario, è essenziale**, etc.).

Bisogna che tu ti **dia** da fare.	*You have to get a move on.*

See the examples in **c)** above. For a more complete list, see unit 18.

2 After certain conjunctions

Often the subjunctive is introduced by a conjunction, or joining word, which links up the two halves of the sentence, expressing purpose, condition, concession or other:

perché, affinché	*in order that*
in modo che, in maniera che	*in such a way that*
purché, a condizione che, a patto che	*on condition that*
benché, sebbene	*although*
comunque	*however*
a meno che	*unless*
prima che	*before*
nel caso che, qualora, caso mai	*if, in case*
nonostante che, malgrado che	*despite*
come se	*as if*

Vengo **a condizione che** tu **inviti** anche Edoardo.
I'll come on condition that you ask Edoardo too.

Me ne vado **a meno che** voi non mi **lasciate** in pace.
I'm going unless you leave me in peace.

Se ne va **senza che** lo salutiamo.
He goes off without us saying goodbye to him.

Sposto la macchina **perché** loro **possano** uscire.
I'll move the car so that they can get out.

Nonostante avessimo sonno, non volevamo perdere la festa.
Although we were sleepy, we didn't want to miss the party.

È **come se** non **capisse** niente.
It's as if he didn't understand anything.

Nel caso veniate in Inghilterra, vi lascio il mio indirizzo.
In case you come to England, I'll leave you my address.

Comunque sia la situazione, non possiamo lasciarlo solo.
Whatever the situation is like, we can't leave him alone.

3 After a superlative (the most, etc.)

After a superlative adjective (*the most, the best, the fastest*, etc.) or an adjective such as **primo** (*first*), **ultimo** (*last*), **unico** or **solo** (*only*) the subjunctive is used in the relative clause (the *'who, which, that'* clause) which follows it:

È la cosa **più bella** che io **abbia** mai visto.	*It's the most beautiful thing I've ever seen.*
È l'**unico** paese che lui non **abbia** mai visitato.	*It's the only country that he's never visited.*
È il libro **meno interessante** che io **abbia** mai letto.	*It's the least interesting book I've ever read.*

4 After certain negatives

After the following negative expressions, the subjunctive is used:

Non è che lui **abbia** tanti soldi.	*It's not that he's got lots of money.*
Non c'è **nessuno che sappia** fare questo.	*There's no-one who knows how to do this.*
Non c'è **niente che desideri** di più.	*There is nothing I would like better.*

5 In restricted relative clauses

Clauses like this usually start with the words *who* or *which*. They are general statements which are then 'limited' or 'restricted' by the relative clause, i.e. a clause beginning with *who, which* or *that*.

(a) Cerco una ragazza inglese.	*I am looking for an English girl.*
(b) Cerco una ragazza **che ami** i bambini.	*I'm looking for a girl who loves children.*
(c) Mary è una ragazza inglese **che ama** i bambini.	*Mary is an English girl who loves children.*

In (a) there is a generalisation: *any* English girl will do. In (b) a restrictive clause is added: any girl *who loves children*. This requires the subjunctive. In (c) one specific girl is mentioned; this does *not* require the subjunctive.

Here are some further examples:

(a) Cerco un registratore a cassette per la macchina.	*I'm looking for a cassette player for the car.*
(b) Cerco un registratore a cassette **che non costi** troppo.	*I'm looking for a cassette player which doesn't cost too much.*
(c) Compro quel registratore a cassette giapponese **che non costa** molto.	*I'm buying that Japanese cassette recorder that doesn't cost much.*

In (a) *any* cassette player for the car is being sought. In (b) any cassette player *that doesn't cost too much*. This restricted type of clause needs the subjunctive. In (c) a specific cassette recorder is mentioned so no subjunctive is necessary.

In the same way, the subjunctive can be found after **qualcuno**:

C'è **qualcuno** che **sappia** parlare cinese? 　　*Is there anyone who can speak Chinese?*

6 After indefinite adjectives or pronouns

qualunque	*whatever, whichever*	**chiunque**	*whoever*
comunque	*however*	**qualsiasi**	*whatever, whichever*

Qualunque cosa **faccia**, è sempre mio figlio. 　　*Whatever he does, he's still my son.*

Chiunque tu sia, non ti permetto di entrare in casa mia. 　　*Whoever you are, I won't allow you to come in to my house.*

Comunque siano le cose, non cambio idea. 　　*Whatever things are like, I won't change my mind.*

Qualsiasi cosa **organizzi**, sbaglia sempre. 　　*Whatever he organises, he always makes mistakes.*

7 When the subordinate or dependent clause comes before the main clause

When the two parts of the sentence are in reverse order, the subjunctive is needed:

Si sa che il progetto non **è** perfetto. 　　*Everyone knows the plan isn't perfect.*

Che il progetto non **sia** perfetto, si sa già. 　　*That the plan isn't perfect, everyone knows already.*

8 As an imperative (order or command)

Normally the subjunctive is found in a subordinate clause (one that depends on something else) but there are a few situations in which it is found as a main verb, standing on its own, for example as an imperative form. To issue a polite request or instruction to someone you are on formal terms with, in Italian, use the subjunctive (**Lei** form, plural **Loro**). This is covered in detail in unit 9.

Venga qui!	*Come here!*
Faccia presto!	*Be quick!*
Dica!	*Tell me!* (what you want)
Dicano, signori!	*Tell me, ladies and gentlemen.*

Language Plus

1 How to avoid the subjunctive

If, after reading units 17,18 and 19, you prefer to avoid using the subjunctive, note the following:

a) Verbs with same subject

Many verbs or verb phrases can be followed directly by the infinitive (**-are, -ere, -ire**) but only if the person in the main part of the sentence is the same person as in the subordinate (dependent) clause. Some examples of this have already been seen in units 17 and 18.

Same subject in both parts of sentence:

Io credo **di avere** poche scarpe.	*I think I have few shoes.*

Different subject:

Teresa crede **che io abbia** troppe scarpe.	*Teresa thinks that I have too many shoes.*

Similar guidelines apply to sentences in the past:

Enrico ritiene **di aver reagito** con calma.	*Enrico maintains he reacted calmly.*
Gli altri ritengono che Enrico **sia stato** preso dal panico.	*The others maintain Enrico was panic-stricken.*

b) Impersonal verbs

In the case of impersonal ('it' verbs), also listed in unit 18, the subjunctive can be avoided if it is a general statement that applies to everyone, i.e. if no specific person is mentioned. If, on the other hand, the statement is 'personalised' and a specific person mentioned, then **che** has to be used, followed by the subjunctive.

Impersonal, general use:

Conviene **partire** presto. *It's best to leave early.*

Personalised, specific person mentioned:

Conviene **che voi partiate** presto. *It's best if you leave early.*

Language in action

Exercise 1

Highlight all the examples of subjunctive in the passage below. Then translate it into English, paying particular attention to the way the subjunctive is used:

Animali abbandonati

(Adapted from *Corriere della Sera*)

Vacanze, tempo di abbandoni. Ogni estate si stima che oltre 25.000 cani e migliaia di altri animali domestici vengano lasciati morire. "In Valtellina – spiega Anna Tosi, volontaria del canile Enpa – riceviamo centinaia di richieste da persone che vogliono che i loro cani vengano tenuti nel nostro Centro." A meno che la situazione non migliori, il randagismo diventerà un pericolo sia per gli uomini che per il bestiame. Qualsiasi provvedimento sia stato varato finora, non ha ottenuto risultati incoraggianti. "La nuova legge appena approvata – aggiunge l'onorevole socialista Dino Mazza – si spera che faccia perdere l'abitudine agli italiani di mettere il cane a dicembre sotto l'albero e ad agosto sull'autostrada." Ma è difficile che questo problema sia risolto facilmente.

Exercise 2

Complete the gaps in this dialogue:

Chiara   A che ora partono Michele e Caterina?

Luciana   È probabile che .... verso le 7.00. I bambini devono salutare i nonni prima di andare via. Almeno Michele vuole che .... i nonni.

Chiara   Sono contenta che .... trovato bel tempo, e che si .... rilassati un poco.

Exercise 3

Rejoice or sympathise

Say whether you are pleased (**sono contento/a**), not pleased (**mi dispiace**) amazed (**sono stupito/a, mi stupisce**) or indifferent (**non mi interessa**) at what your friend tells you. Remember that verbs expressing emotion require the subjunctive, either past or present:

e.g. Ti piace Giorgio? È fidanzato!
　　 Mi dispiace che **sia** fidanzato.

1　La Scozia ha vinto la partita e gioca contro l'Italia stasera.
2　Domani c'è sciopero. Non ci sono lezioni.
3　Mia madre è caduta. Si è rotta il braccio.
4　Il mio cane è stato investito da una macchina.
5　L'insegnante boccia Giovanni all'esame di storia contemporanea.
6　Stasera mia zia prepara la pasta con le vongole.
7　Mio fratello mi ha preso in prestito il CD nuovo e l'ha graffiato.
8　Viene anche la mia ex-ragazza stasera.
9　I miei genitori mi danno L100.000 per il mio compleanno.
10　Mio padre mi offre un viaggio a Parigi per festeggiare l'onomastico.
11　Gianna deve stare a dieta perché è ingrassata di 5 kg.
12　Fra me e il calcio, il mio ragazzo preferisce il calcio.

20 | EXPRESSING WISHES OR POLITE REQUESTS

Learn how to ...

■ Express a wish for yourself ■ Express a wish involving someone else ■ Make a polite request ■ Allow someone to do something ■ Get someone to do something ■ Order, suggest, invite, encourage someone to do something

Language points

■ Conditional **vorrei** to express a wish or request ■ **Vorrei + che +** imperfect subjunctive ■ Conditional used to express polite request ■ Other uses of the conditional ■ Other uses of the imperfect subjunctive ■ **chiedere, ordinare a qualcuno di** ■ Using **fare, lasciare** and infinitive

Introduction

Look at these examples of statements expressing a wish or polite request:

Vorrei mangiare fuori stasera.	*I should like to eat out tonight.*
Vorrei che lui non fosse così ostinato.	*I wish he were not so stubborn.*
Le dispiacerebbe aprire la finestra?	*Would you mind opening the window?*
Ci chiede di non fumare.	*She asks us not to smoke.*

Focus on grammar

1 Expressing a wish (using the conditional and subjunctive)

Units 17, 18 and 19 showed how the subjunctive is used after verbs of emotion, hoping, or fearing; it must also be used after verbs of wishing (e.g. **volere**) and requesting (e.g. **chiedere**) where another person is involved. If you are expressing a wish for yourself, **voglio** or **vorrei** can be followed directly by the infinitive (see unit 14 for further examples.) But when we wish that *someone else* would do something, **voglio** or **vorrei** have to be followed by **che** then the subjunctive. Look at these two examples:

Domani **voglio lavare** la macchina. *Tomorrow I want to wash the car.*
Domani **voglio che** mio marito *Tomorrow I want my husband to*
   lavi la macchina. *wash the car.*

Frequently verbs of wishing are expressed in the conditional form (*I would like*, etc.) and are followed by the *imperfect* tense of the subjunctive rather than the *present* tense:

Vorrei che tu mi **portassi** fuori *I would like you to take me out*
   ogni tanto. *every so often.*

Vorrebbe che Lei gli **telefonasse**. *He would like you to telephone*
   him.

When a wish is expressed that the action had or hadn't taken place, the *pluperfect* tense of the subjunctive is used:

Desidererei che non **fosse** mai *I wish this had never happened*
   successa questa cosa. (Lit: *I would like for this thing*
   never to have happened.)

See unit 21 for further examples of this.

2 How to form the conditional

The conditional in English is expressed by the words *would, should*. It is called 'conditional' because the statement will only become fact *on condition that something happens*. The forms of the Italian **condizionale** or conditional, a verb mood, are given below. The forms of the present conditional vary little from verb to verb. They are formed by taking the infinitive (**-are, -ere, -ire**), dropping the final **-e**, and adding the conditional endings shown below. The **-are** verbs change the **-a-** of **-are** to **-e-**.

Conditional endings

-ei, -esti, -ebbe, -emmo, -este, ebbero

Verbs ending in *-are*

parlare	
parler**ei**	parler**emmo**
parler**esti**	parler**este**
parler**ebbe**	parler**ebbero**

Verbs ending in *-ere*

mettere	
metter**ei**	metter**emmo**
metter**esti**	metter**este**
metter**ebbe**	metter**ebbero**

Verbs ending in -ire

partire	
partir**ei**	partir**emmo**
partir**esti**	partir**este**
partir**ebbe**	partir**ebbero**

3 When to use the conditional

a) To express a wish

Vorrei un panino con prosciutto.   *I would like a ham sandwich.*

More examples can be found in unit 14.

b) To express a request more politely

Le **dispiacerebbe** passarmi la valigia?

Would you mind passing me my suitcase?

Potrei venire più tardi?	*Could I come later?*
Potrebbe prestarmi il suo orario?	*Could you lend me your timetable?*
Mi **farebbe** una cortesia?	*Could you do me a favour?*

The phrase **fare una cortesia** can be replaced by **fare un piacere** or **fare un favore**.

c) To make a statement sound less categorical

Non **saprei** spiegartelo.	*I wouldn't know how to explain it to you.*
Dovrei scrivere delle cartoline.	*I ought to write some postcards.*

Compare this last sentence with:

Devo mandare delle cartoline.	*I must send some postcards.*

d) To express rumour, hearsay or report

The conditional is often used to tell us what someone said, or what was written in the press. It is translated by a straightforward present indicative in English.

Secondo la stampa, il governo **sarebbe** contrario.	*According to the press, the government is against it.*
Secondo Gianni, Maria **avrebbe** più di 40 anni.	*According to Gianni, Maria is over 40.*

e) When a condition is implied or stated

You use the conditional when your action is dependent on certain conditions being fulfilled; sometimes these conditions are stated; sometimes they are just implied. (See unit 22 for further examples of conditional sentences.)

Andrei in vacanza ma non ho soldi.	*I would go on holiday but I don't have any money.*
Io **partirei** subito.	*I would leave straightaway.*

(An *if* condition is implied – such as *if I were you, if I were able*)

Se avessi i soldi, **comprerei** una macchina nuova.	*If I had the money, I would buy a new car.*

f) Indirect or reported speech or after a verb of saying, thinking, etc.

Dice che **verrebbe** domani. *He says he would come tomorrow.*

Penso che **sarebbe** meglio partire domani. *I think it would be better to leave tomorrow.*

To see what happens when the sentence is in the past tense, see unit 21.

4 How to form the imperfect subjunctive

The imperfect subjunctive is formed by taking the stem of the infinitive, i.e. the infinitive without the final **-are, -ere, -ire**, then adding a set of endings, e.g. parl**are** – parl**assi**. When giving the subjunctive forms, we usually start with the word **che** since it is rare for the subjunctive to stand on its own. Here are the forms of the imperfect subjunctive for the three main groups of verbs:

parlare	e.g. **che io parlassi**
parl**assi**	parl**assimo**
parl**assi**	parl**aste**
parl**asse**	parl**assero**

mettere	e.g. **che io mettessi**
mett**essi**	mett**essimo**
mett**essi**	mett**este**
mett**esse**	mett**essero**

partire	e.g. **che io partissi**
part**issi**	part**issimo**
part**issi**	part**iste**
part**isse**	part**issero**

There are only a few verbs which vary from this pattern. They include the following:

bere	*to drink*	(che) io **bevessi**
essere	*to be*	(che) io **fossi**
stare	*to be*	(che) io **stessi**
fare	*to do*	(che) io **facessi**
dire	*to say*	(che) io **dicessi**
dare	*to give*	(che) io **dessi**

5 When to use the imperfect subjunctive

The imperfect subjunctive is often used after the following tenses in the main clause: *imperfect*, *conditional*, but can also be used after the ***passato remoto***, the *perfect* or *pluperfect* tense, the *past conditional* and occasionally the *present*.

a) After the imperfect

Mio marito **aveva** paura che l'albergo **fosse** troppo caro.

My husband was afraid that the hotel was too dear.

b) After the conditional

Sarebbe meglio che tu non mi **chiedessi** questo.

It would be better if you didn't ask me this.

c) After the passato remoto

Il terrorista **si lanciò** dalla finestra perché la polizia non lo **prendesse**.

The terrorist threw himself out of the window so that the police would not get him.

d) After the perfect

La signora ci **ha chiesto** se **ci trovassimo** bene in Italia.

The lady asked us if we were enjoying Italy.

e) After the pluperfect

L'impiegata ci **aveva chiesto** se **volessimo** un biglietto di andata e ritorno.

The ticket clerk had asked us if we wanted a return ticket.

f) After the past conditional

Non **avrei** mai **pensato** che tu potessi fare una cosa del genere.	*I should never have thought that you could do a thing like that.*

g) After the present

Penso che l'autista **avesse** qualche problema.	*I think the driver had some problem or other.*

Language plus

There are other ways in which you can ask someone to do something without using the subjunctive. Generally these are combinations of verb and the person being asked and the action that the person is being asked to carry out, with or without prepositions linking these different elements.

1 Chiedere, ordinare a qualcuno di fare qualcosa

Verbs such as **chiedere, ordinare** use **a** to link with the person being given the instruction, then **di** to link with the infinitive expressing the action the person is being asked to carry out:

Chiedo *al* **cameriere** *di* **portare il menù.**	*I'll ask the waiter to bring the menu.*
I tedeschi **hanno ordinato** *alla* cameriera *di* portare cinque birre.	*The Germans ordered the waitress to bring five beers.*

Instead of naming the person directly (**al cameriere, alla cameriera**), you can use the indirect pronouns **mi, ti, gli** (*to me, to you, to him*) etc. The examples above would then become:

Gli chiedo di portare il menù.	*I'll ask him to bring the menu.*
I tedeschi **le** hanno ordinato di portare cinque birre.	*The Germans ordered her to bring five beers.*

Other verbs used in this way include verbs of advising such as **consigliare, dire, suggerire** and verbs of permitting or allowing such as **consentire, permettere**:

Cosa **ci consigli di** fare?	*What do you advise us to do?*
Non **permette agli** ospiti **di** usare la doccia dopo le 8.00.	*She doesn't allow guests to use the shower after 8 o'clock.*

Il suo contributo **mi ha consentito di** completare la ricerca.		*His contribution allowed me to finish my research.*	
Il padrone del ristorante **ha detto ai** clienti **di** scegliere quello che volevano.		*The owner of the restaurant told the customers to choose what they wanted.*	

Here are some of the commonest verbs of this type, in alphabetical order:

chiedere	*to ask*	ordinare	*to order*
comandare	*to command*	permettere	*to permit*
consentire	*to allow*	proibire	*to forbid*
consigliare	*to advise*	promettere	*to promise*
dire	*to say, tell*	ricordare	*to remind*
domandare	*to ask*	suggerire	*to suggest*
impedire	*to prevent*	vietare	*to forbid*

In addition, there are a few verbs which are linked to the infinitive by **a**:

Ti insegno a fare in windsurf.   *I'll teach you to windsurf.*

2 Invitare, convincere qualcuno a fare qualcosa

Some verbs are followed directly by the person being given the instruction, then by **a** and the infinitive:

Hanno invitato mio marito **a** fare una conferenza.   *They have invited my husband to give a lecture.*

In this case, the pronoun if used must be the direct object pronoun: **mi, ti, lo, la, ci, vi, li, le**:

Mi ha invitata a venire al mare con lui.   *He invited me to come to the seaside with him.*

Ti ha convinta a comprare quella borsa?   *Did he persuade you to buy that bag?*

Here are some more verbs that act in a similar way:

aiutare	*to help*	incoraggiare	*to encourage*
costringere	*to force*	invitare	*to invite*
convincere	*to persuade*	obbligare	*to oblige*
forzare	*to force*	persuadere	*to persuade*

3 fare, lasciare, sentire, vedere qualcuno fare qualcosa

Other verbs can be followed directly by the person and then directly by the infinitive. Again the pronoun, if used, must be a direct object pronoun:

Lasciare fare (*to allow, let, make someone do something*):

La lascia salire sul treno senza biglietto.	*He lets her get on the train without a ticket.*
Mi ha fatto salire senza biglietto.	*He let me get on without a ticket.*

Sentire (*to hear*), **vedere** (*to see*)

L'ho visto salire sul treno.	*I saw him get on the train.*
L'ho sentito entrare.	*I heard him come in.*

Finally, look at the difference between the following examples: in examples (a) the verb is followed directly by the infinitive, while in examples (b) **che** and the subjunctive have been used:

a) Chiedo a Gianna **di venire** con noi.	*I ask Gianna to come with us.*
b) Chiedo **che** Gianna **venga** con noi.	*I ask (someone, not necessarily Gianna herself) that Gianna comes with us (if Gianna can come with us).*
a) Marco mi chiede **di pagare**.	*Marco asks me to pay.*
b) Marco chiede **che** io **paghi**.	*Marco asks that I pay.*
a) Non permette a suo marito **di uscire** la sera.	*She doesn't allow her husband to go out in the evening.*
b) Non permette **che** suo marito **esca** la sera.	*She doesn't allow her husband to go out in the evening.*

Language in action

Exercise 1

Expressing a polite request

Ask someone to do something politely, using the present conditional, as illustrated above. We have provided some clues as well as the verb you need. The rest is up to you.

1	*(Someone is stepping on your foot)*	**spostare**
2	*(The room is very stuffy)*	**aprire**

3 *(Someone has left the door open and there is a draught)* **chiudere**
4 *(You can't reach the sugar, it's near the man opposite)* **passare**
5 *(You've forgotten your pen and need to fill in a form)* **prestare**
6 *(You need to know the time)* **dire**
7 *(You need to borrow L20.000 off your friend)* **prestare**
8 *(You need some help in moving something)* **dare una mano**

Exercise 2

In this passage underline or highlight all the verbs in the subjunctive, as well as the verb, verb phrase, conjunction or other structure that they depend on. Then translate it into English.

Sleeping over at my grandmother's

Era strano quel che succedeva quando dormivo con mia nonna...quando mi risvegliavo, mi ritrovavo nella stessa posizione... Penso che mia nonna si svegliasse molto prima di me e mi risistemasse nella stessa posizione, ma era bello immaginare che avessimo dormito in quella posizione per tutta la notte. In ogni caso era bellissimo che lei facesse di tutto per farmelo credere.

From Lara Cardella: *Volevo i pantaloni* (Edizioni Oscar Originals).

Exercise 3

In the following passage the highlighted constructions require the verb following to be in the subjunctive. The infinitive of these verbs is supplied. Work out which form of the subjunctive is required and fill it in.

My past life in Milan

Ogni tanto andavo a casa di Bruno ed **era facile che** (*restare*) fino alle due di notte a chiacchierare, perché era **l'unica** persona con cui io (*potere*) parlare liberamente. Lui **voleva che** io gli (*parlare*) in inglese, perché stava studiando la lingua, ma io non mi sentivo più a mio agio **nonostante** (*essere*) la mia madre lingua. Mia madre non sapeva né mi chiedeva mai **con chi** (*uscire*) e **lasciava** che io (*prendere*) la macchina senza farmi domande di nessun tipo.

21 | **EXPRESSING REGRETS**

Learn how to ...

■ Express regrets ■ Say you are sorry ■ Talk about an action which would have taken place (if)… ■ Express hearsay ■ Express reported speech

Language points

■ **Vorrei** followed by **che** and the pluperfect subjunctive ■ Other ways of using pluperfect subjunctive ■ Past conditional used after **ha detto che**

Introduction

When expressing a wish that the action had or hadn't taken place, the *pluperfect* tense of the subjunctive is used:

Preferirebbe che io l'avessi avvertito.	*He would prefer me to have warned him.*
Vorrei che non fossimo mai venuti.	*I wish that we had never come.*
Avrei voluto che non fossimo mai venuti.	*I would have liked us never to have come.*
Avrebbe preferito che la mamma avesse preparato le polpettine.	*He would have preferred his mum to have prepared meatballs.*

In a simple sentence, however, involving only the speaker, the verb, whether in the conditional or past conditional, can be followed directly by the infinitive:

Avrebbe voluto non esserci.	*He would have liked not to be there.*
Avremmo voluto vederlo.	*We would like to have seen it.*

| Preferirei non essere qui in questo momento. | *I would prefer not to be here right now.* |

Now read the Focus on grammar section for details.

Focus on grammar

1 How to form the pluperfect subjunctive

The pluperfect subjunctive is formed by combining the imperfect subjunctive of **avere** or **essere** (whichever the verb normally takes) and the appropriate past participle, e.g. **mangiato, bevuto, partito**:

Vorrebbe che ...	
avessi mangiato	**avessimo** mangiato
avessi mangiato	**aveste** mangiato
avesse mangiato	**avessero** mangiato

Vorrebbe che ...	
fossi venuto/a	**fossimo** venuti/e
fossi venuto/a	**foste** venuti/e
fosse venuto/a	**fossero** venuti/e

2 When to use the pluperfect subjunctive

The pluperfect subjunctive is generally used after a verb such as **pensare** to express something that someone had or hadn't done. Look at these pairs of examples: in the first example of each pair, the pluperfect *indicative* (the normal verb form) is used; in the second of each pair, the pluperfect *subjunctive* is used:

With *avere*

| **Avevi** già **assaggiato** la pasta con le vongole? | *Had you already tried pasta with clams?* |
| **Pensavo** che **tu avessi** già **assaggiato** la pasta con le vongole. | *I thought you had already tried pasta with clams.* |

With *essere*

Eri già **stata** a Pompei?	*Had you already been to Pompei?*
Pensavo che **tu fossi** già stata a Pompei.	*I thought you had already been to Pompei.*

3 How to form the past conditional

In unit 20, we saw the conditional used to express a wish or to put a request more politely. The past conditional is used in a similar way.

Whereas the conditional is expressed in English by the words *would* or *should*, the past conditional is expressed by the words *would have* or *should have*. It is formed in Italian by using the conditional of **avere** (or **essere** in the case of verbs that use **essere** in the past) with the past participle (the **-ato, -ito, -uto** form):

Verbs in *-are*

avrei mangiato	**avremmo** mangiato
avresti mangiato	**avreste** mangiato
avrebbe mangiato	**avrebbero** mangiato

Verbs in -ere

avrei potuto	**avremmo** potuto
avresti potuto	**avreste** potuto
avrebbe potuto	**avrebbero** potuto

Verbs in *-ire*

avrei dormito	**avremmo** dormito
avresti dormito	**avreste** dormito
avrebbe dormito	**avrebbero** dormito

Verbs that take *essere*, e.g. *andare*

sarei andato/a	**saremmo** andati/e
saresti andato/a	**sareste** andati/e
sarebbe andato/a	**sarebbero** andati/e

In the case of verbs that take **essere**, the participle must change ending depending on whether the subject is masculine, or feminine, singular or plural.

4 When to use the past conditional

a) To express a wish

Avrei preferito una granita. *I would have preferred a granita (water ice.)*

Avrei voluto una persona più esperta. *I would have liked someone more experienced.*

b) To make a statement or question sound less categorical or abrupt

Non avresti avuto tempo di guardare quella relazione per caso? *You wouldn't have had time to look at that report by any chance?*

c) To express rumour or hearsay

The past conditional is used to say what has happened, according to a certain source, e.g. press, TV, and is translated in English by a straightforward past tense:

Secondo fonti ufficiali, 35 persone **sarebbero state uccise** negli scontri fra le due fazioni. *According to official sources, 35 people have been killed in the clashes between the two parties.*

d) When a condition is implied or stated

Use the past conditional when the action would have taken place *if* certain conditions had been fulfilled. Sometimes these conditions are stated; at other times they are just implied.

Sarei andato in vacanza, ma non
avevo i soldi.

*I would have gone on holiday but
I didn't have the money.*

Sarei venuta anch'io.   *I would have come too.*
(Here, a condition is implied e.g. *If I had known about it*)

Io non avrei comprato quella casa. *I wouldn't have bought that house.*
(The condition implied is: *If it had been me ...*)

e) Indirect or reported speech, or after a verb of saying, thinking, etc.

Ha detto che **sarebbe venuto**
domani.

*He said he would have come
tomorrow.*

*Or He said he would come
tomorrow.*

In the example above, English would use the *present* conditional. But
after a main verb in the past, Italian uses the *past* conditional.

Language plus

1 Other expressions of regret

Che peccato!   *What a pity! What a shame!*

Che peccato che lui non **abbia
potuto** finire il corso di laurea.
Che peccato che voi non **siate
potuti** venire/ **abbiate potuto**
venire.

*What a pity that he couldn't
finish his degree course.*
*What a shame that you couldn't
come.*

Mi dispiace   *I am sorry*

Mi dispiace che non ci **siamo**
più **visti**.

*I'm sorry that we haven't seen
each other again.*

Sono desolato   *I'm really sorry*

Sono desolato che lui non ti
abbia più **telefonato**.

*I'm really sorry that he hasn't
rung you anymore.*

Language in action

Exercise 1

Nando is having car problems. Fill in the gaps, this time with the correct form of the subjunctive, either imperfect, perfect or pluperfect, and make any necessary adjustments.

Andrea   Ciao, Nando, **pensavo** che tu (*partire*) per la Spagna.

Nando   No, invece abbiamo avuto dei problemi con la macchina. Il meccanico ci aveva fatto la manutenzione e ha detto che era tutto a posto ma **è impossibile** che la (*controllare*) per bene, perché dopo neanche duecento metri si è fermata e non è più partita. Magari non la (*portare*) mai da lui!

Andrea   Ma vi fidavate di questo meccanico? Lo conoscevate già?

Nando   Noi non **sapevamo** se (*essere*) bravo o no. Dei nostri amici avevano portato la macchina da lui, e ci avevano detto che era bravo, **benché** (*fare*) pagare un prezzo un po' salato. E poi ci ha riparato la macchina subito, **senza che** (*dovere*) aspettare.

Andrea   **Era meglio** invece se (*aspettare*)!

Exercise 2

Soggiorno a Venezia

Read this brief account of a holiday in Venice that didn't go according to plan. Highlight all the subjunctive forms and the verbs or other constructions that they depend on. Then translate the whole passage into English, paying particular attention to the subjunctives.

La vita è piena di sbagli. Noi avevamo prenotato l'albergo a Venezia su consiglio di un'amica. Non sapevamo che lei non fosse mai stata a Venezia, e che il nome dell'albergo l'avesse trovato su una vecchia guida turistica. Sarà stato bello cinquanta anni fa, ma non più. E il ristorante poi....! Morivamo di sete! Nonostante avessimo detto al cameriere tre volte di portare del vino rosso, ha portato solo acqua minerale. Peccato poi che il cuoco abbia dimenticato di togliere lo spago prima di servire l'arrosto... mi chiedevo poi perché mio marito avesse deciso di mangiarlo, ma lui, poveretto, aveva pensato che il cuoco avesse preparato una specialità tipica e che lo spago ne fosse una parte essenziale. Avremmo mangiato meglio alla mensa degli studenti – e avremmo anche speso di meno.

22 | EXPRESSING CONDITIONS

Learn how to ...

■ Express a condition that can be met ■ Express a condition unlikely to be met ■ Express a condition that can no longer be met

Language points

■ **se** used with present/future/past tenses to express a condition that can be met, or a simple statement of fact. ■ **se** used with imperfect subjunctive and present conditional to express a condition or hypothesis that is unlikely to be met ■ **se** used with pluperfect subjunctive and past conditional to express a condition or hypothesis that can no longer be met ■ Phrases that express a condition (**a condizione che, a meno che**; etc.)

Introduction

Study these different examples of conditional sentences before reading the grammar explanations:

Se ho tempo, scrivo delle cartoline.	*If I have time, I write postcards.*
Se verrà Marco, andremo al cinema.	*If Marco comes, we will go to the cinema.*
Se fossi ricca, comprerei una Rolls Royce.	*If I were rich, I would buy a Rolls Royce.*
Se avessimo tempo, andremmo a visitare la cattedrale.	*If we had time, we would go and visit the cathedral.*
Se avessi sposato un italiano, avrei dovuto imparare l'italiano.	*If I had married an Italian, I would have had to learn Italian.*

Se avessimo comprato la guida, non avremmo avuto tanti problemi per trovare un buon ristorante.	*If we had bought the guide, we would not have had so many problems finding a good restaurant.*

Focus on grammar

1 Conditional sentences: introduction

When we start a sentence with *if* in English, we are laying down a condition (*If you do or don't do something, then something will or won't happen*). This can be one of many kinds:

A straightforward statement of fact or condition which can easily be met:

If you stay up late, you will be tired tomorrow.
If we have time, we will go and see the Duomo.

A condition unlikely ever to be met:

If I were to become rich, I would buy a Rolls Royce.

A condition that can no longer be met, because the time or opportunity has passed:

If I had married Giovanni, I would have had an Italian mother-in-law.

Here we show how these different ideas are expressed in Italian.

2 Conditions that can or might be met, simple statements of fact

Where a straightforward statement of facts is involved, the indicative (the normal verb form) is used for both verbs, in the appropriate tense:

Present

Se Lei mi **dà** L.100.000, io Le **do** il resto.	*If you give me L.100,000, I'll give you the change.*

Future

Se andrete a Roma, **potrete** vedere il Colosseo.	*If you go to Rome, you will be able to see the Colosseum.*

Past

Se **aveva** paura, non lo **dimostrava**.

If she was afraid, she didn't show it.

Combination of present and future

Se non **fai** il bravo, non **andrai** al mare domani.

If you don't behave, you won't go to the seaside tomorrow.

Combination of perfect and future perfect

Se **hai parlato** con lui, **avrai capito** come stanno le cose.

If you have spoken to him, you will have understood how things are.

Combination of present and imperative

Se **vieni**, **fammi** sapere.

If you come, let me know.

3 Conditions that are unlikely to be met

Where the condition expressed is unlikely to be fulfilled, the *if* clause (conditional clause) is expressed by **se** and the *imperfect subjunctive*, while the action or event which would happen (the main clause) is expressed by the *present conditional*:

Se l'albergo non **fosse** così caro, **resteremmo** più di una notte.

If the hotel were less dear, we would stay more than one night.

Se **avessimo** più soldi, **andremmo** a mangiare al ristorante.

If we had more money, we would go and eat in a restaurant.

Se gli italiani **guidassero** con più attenzione, non **farebbero** tanti incidenti.

If the Italians drove more carefully, they wouldn't have so many accidents.

4 Conditions that cannot now be met

When the condition or hypothesis expressed cannot now be fulfilled because the opportunity has passed, the *if* clause uses **se** and the *pluperfect subjunctive*, while the main clause (the action or event which would have happened) is expressed in the *past conditional*:

'If' clause

Se io non **avessi perso** il portafoglio… *If I had not lost my wallet...*

Main clause

… non **avrei avuto** tutti questi   *… I wouldn't have had all these*
problemi.   *problems.*

'If' clause and main clause

Se fossimo venuti in treno,   *If we had come by train, we*
  saremmo arrivati prima. *would have got here sooner.*
Se tu avessi guidato con più   *If you had driven more carefully,*
  prudenza, non **saremmo andati** *we would not have ended up*
  a finire contro il muro.   *crashing into the wall.*

The past conditional can also be used after a gerund (**-ando**, or **-endo**) where the idea of *if* is implied:

Sapendo questo, **non sarei**   *If I had known this, I wouldn't*
  andata con lui.   *have gone with him.*

5 Phrases expressing condition

A few conjunctions (joining words) that express condition are:

a condizione che   *on condition that*
a meno che   *unless*
purché   *provided that*

All these conjunctions are followed by a verb in the subjunctive (see unit 19):

Io ti ci accompagno **a condizione**   *I'll take you there on condition*
  che tu paghi la benzina.   *that you pay for the petrol.*
Potete uscire **purché non**   *You can go out so long as you*
  rientriate troppo tardi. *don't come back too late.*
Possiamo andare al mare **a meno**   *We can go to the seaside unless*
  che Lei non preferisca andare *you prefer to go to the country.*
  in campagna.

Language Plus

1 Conditional sentence using the imperfect

Often in a hypothetical sentence such as those shown in 3 above, both
past conditional and *pluperfect subjunctive* are replaced by a simple
imperfect indicative in spoken Italian:

Se lo **avessi saputo**, non **sarei venuta** stasera.
Se lo **sapev**o, non **venivo** stasera.   *If I had known, I wouldn't have
come this evening.*

Occasionally only the *if* clause is replaced by an imperfect:

Se **sapevo**, non **sarei venuta**   *If I had known, I wouldn't have
stasera.   come this evening.*

Language in action

Exercise 1

Next time ...

Supply the missing half! Conditional sentences are generally a pair
formed by a **se** clause and a main clause, but in this dialogue one of each
pair is missing. Using the verbs supplied below, try and complete the
sentence by making up the missing half.

Verbs to be used: **essere, fare, invitare, venire** (some may be used more
than once).

Carla   Ciao, Maria. Come mai non sei venuta stasera?
Maria   .... **se non avessi avuto** tante altre cose da fare.
Carla   Peccato. **Se tu** .... **ti avrei fatto** conoscere mio cugino.
Maria   Pazienza! Sarà per la prossima volta. **Se lui** .... per Natale,
           fammi sapere.
Carla   Non mancherò. Intanto **se tu non** ....**sempre** così
           impegnata **ti inviterei** a cena.
Maria   **Se mi** ...., **accetto** volentieri!

Note:

Pazienza!   *Never mind! Can't be helped.* (Literally *patience!*)

Exercise 2

Still time ...

In this set of examples, there is still the chance to change your destiny!

1   Se mia madre sapessse cucinare .... *(mangiare meglio)*
2   Se mio padre fosse meno rigido .... *(uscire tutte le sere, fare quello che voglio)*
3   Se vivessimo in una casa più grande .... *(avere una camera tutta mia)*
4   Se tu abitassi più vicino a casa mia .... *(vederci più spesso)*
5   Se mio fratello fosse vegetariano .... *(non mangiare la carne)*

Exercise 3

If only...

What might have happened if you or your friends had done things differently? Let's see. Some suggestions are supplied but you are free to make up your own.

1   Se io avessi sposato un italiano ....
    (rimanere in Italia, parlare italiano meglio, avere una vita più felice)
2   Se noi avessimo studiato i verbi ....
    (essere più bravi, avere un voto migliore)
3   Se tu fossi andata all'Università ....
    (divertirsi, trovare un lavoro migliore)
4   Se lei avesse messo il vestito più bello ....
    (conoscere l'uomo dei suoi sogni ...)
5. Se lui non avesse bevuto tanto ....
    (andare a finire contro un muro, distruggere la macchina)

KEY TO EXERCISES

Unit 1

Exercise 1, scene 4

Ciao, Valentina. Questa è Mary, **la mia amica inglese**. / Ciao Mary. Io sono Daniela, questo è Hans. / Piacere. Io sono Hans, sono **un turista tedesco** di Monaco di Baviera. / Scusa, Valentina, il tuo ragazzo come si chiama? / Io sono James, **uno studente inglese**.

Exercise 2

1. Mi chiamo Tracey Jones. Sono inglese, di Milton Keynes. Sono studentessa. 2. Mi chiamo Massimiliano Lusardi. Sono italiano, di Genova. Sono studente. 3. Mi chiamo Dottor Barnes. Sono di Oxford ma sono gallese. Sono professore universitario. 4. Mi chiamo Camilla Pennino. Sono italiana, di Roma. Sono medico.

Exercise 3

1. È tedesco. 2. È gallese. 3. Sono scozzesi. 4. È irlandese. 5. Sono italiani. 6. Sono austriaci. 7. Sono americani. 8. Sono inglesi.

Unit 2

Exercise 1

un cornetto; **un** caffè; **una** spremuta; **una** birra; **un** cappuccino; **una** brioche; **un'**aranciata; **un** aperitivo; **un** toast; **una** limonata; **un** digestivo; **un** bicchiere di acqua minerale

Exercise 2

due cornetti; due caffè; due spremute; due birre; due cappuccini; due brioche; due aranciate; due aperitivi; due toast; due limonate; due digestivi; due bicchieri di acqua minerale

Exercise 3

1. Due cappuccini e un cornetto. 2. Un aperitivo, un'aranciata e due toast. 3. Un caffè, una spremuta e due cornetti. 4. Una birra, una coca cola e un bicchiere di acqua minerale. 5. Due caffè e un bicchiere di acqua. 6. Due coni.

Unit 3

Exercise 1

Dei salatini; delle patatine; delle pastine; degli stuzzicchini; dei grissini; delle pizzette; degli spuntini; delle bibite; degli aperitivi; della coca cola; dell'aranciata; del vino; della birra; degli alcolici; degli analcolici; delle uova sode; dell'acqua; dei liquori; del gelato; del dolce.

Alcuni salatini/qualche salatino; alcune patatine/qualche patatina; alcune pastine/qualche pastina; alcuni stuzzicchini/qualche stuzzicchino; alcuni grissini/qualche grissino; alcune pizzette/qualche pizzetta; alcuni spuntini/qualche spuntino; alcuni aperitivi/qualche aperitivo; un po' di coca-cola; un po' di aranciata; un po' di vino; un po' di birra; alcuni alcolici / qualche alcolico; alcune uova sode / qualche uovo sodo; un po' di acqua; alcuni liquori / qualche liquore; un po' di gelato; un po' di dolce.

Exercise 2

1. Ce ne sono dieci. 2. Ce n'è un litro. 3. Ce ne sono sei bottiglie. 4. Ce n'è un chilo. 5. Ce ne sono due buste.

Unit 4

Exercise 1

1. Il latte è **nel** frigorifero. 2. Le tazzine sono **nell'**armadietto **in** cucina. 3. L'impianto stereo è **nel** soggiorno. 4. Il gatto è **nel / in** giardino. 5. La lavatrice è **nel / in** bagno. 6. Le lenzuola sono **nel** cassettone. 7. Il telecomando è vicino **alla** poltrona. 8. I libri italiani sono **nella** camera degli ospiti. 9. I dizionari sono **sullo** scaffale **nello** studio. 10. Le chiavi sono **nel** cassetto della credenza.

Exercise 2

1. Sono in Via Roma, vicino all'Orto Botanico. 2. È in Piazza del Duomo, vicino alla Torre Pendente. 3. Sono in Via Alessandro Volta, vicino al Museo di Storia Naturale. 4. È in Via Nicola Pisano, vicino alle cliniche universitarie. 5. È in Via Antonio Rosmini, vicino allo Stadio Garibaldi. 6. È in Piazza Manin, vicino al Battistero.

Unit 5

Exercise 1

1. Preferisco quella in campagna / in città. 2. Prendo quella economica / cara. 3. Metto quelli sportivi / eleganti. 4. Compro quelle con tacco alto / senza tacco. 5. Metto quelli da L650 / da L850. 6. Prendo quello con prosciutto / con formaggio. 7. Mangio quelli con nocciola / con cioccolato. 8. Bevo quello rosso / bianco. 9. Leggo quello inglese / italiano. 10. Guardo quelli comici / romantici.

Exercise 2

1. Quell'aranciata è tiepida. 2. Quel palazzo è lontano. 3. Quegli studenti sono stupidi. 4. Quell'albergo è scadente. 5. Quei giornalisti sono disonesti. 6. Quella bottiglia è vuota. 7. Quel film è noioso. 8. Quel museo è aperto. 9. Quello straniero è antipatico. 10. Quello specialista è giovane.

Unit 6

Exercise 1

Il signor Ruzzini comincia a lavorare alle otto e quindici. Abita a Pisa ma lavora a Firenze. Ogni giorno prende il treno. Parte alle sette e arriva alle otto.

Exercise 2

La signora Giannini lavora in centro. Comincia alle otto e trenta e finisce alle sette. Quando torna a casa, è stanca morta. Suo marito non lavora ma resta a casa con la bambina. La sera lei e suo marito guardano la tv.

Exercise 3

Vieni al cinema, Marco? / Sì, vengo volentieri. / Sbrigati, allora, **usciamo** proprio adesso. / **Vengo**. Mi **metto** le scarpe. / Sei sempre l'ultimo. / **Scherzi**! Tu sei la più lenta di tutti.

Exercise 4

N Noi andiamo in/Voi andate in.

N … partiamo da …/. Arriviamo a …/Torniamo a.

N Malcolm studia./Alexè./Fa molta./Ha molti./Va al cinema.

N Anna è …/. Torna a casa/È stressata/Finisce il.

Exercise 5

1. Sto preparando / facendo un tè. 2. Sto andando a noleggiare la macchina. 3. Stiamo portando il cane a spasso / portandolo a spasso. 4. Sto riparando la radio / sto riparandola. 5. Sto scrivendo un romanzo. 6. Mi sto tagliando le unghie. 7. Sto partendo. 8. Sto bevendo un caffè. 9. Sto facendo una foto della nuova casa. 10. Sto traducendo una lettera.

Unit 7

Exercise 1

Piero e Maddalena, perché non andate a **farvi** la doccia? Su, cercate di **sbrigarvi**! Poi **mettetevi** i vestiti puliti e **pettinatevi** un pochino. Bevete il latte, mangiate i biscotti poi andate a **lavarvi** i denti. **Mettetevi** le scarpe e la giacca, che fa freddo. / Serafino, vai a fare la doccia, **sbrigati**! Metti la camicia bianca e la cravatta azzurra. Bevi il caffè, mangia qualcosa! Mettiti il cappello!

Exercise 2

1. Preferisco **farmi** prima la doccia. 2. Preferisco **prendere** prima il caffè. 3. Preferisco **mettermi** prima i calzini. 4. Preferisco **pettinarmi** prima. 5. Preferisco **lavarmi** prima i capelli. 6. Preferisco **lavarmi** prima i denti.

Exercise 3

(Free choice exercise)

La mattina mio marito si alza prima di me e mi prepara il caffè. Io mi alzo dopo, mi faccio la doccia, mi lavo i capelli, mi vesto e poi mi preparo ad uscire. Dopo colazione, mi trucco, mi lavo i denti, mi metto le scarpe, mi pettino un'altra volta poi esco. Mio marito invece si fa la doccia, si veste, si lava i denti, si pettina e si fa la barba. Poi si mette le scarpe ed esce.

Unit 8

Exercise 1

1. ho potuto. 2. hanno potuto/potevano. 3. ho potuto. 4. potevamo. 5. ho potuto. 6. abbiamo potuto.

Exercise 2

1. Potrebbe. 2. Potrebbe. 3. Potrebbero. 4. Potresti. 5. Potresti. 6. Potreste. 7. Potrebbe. 8. Potrei.

Exercise 3

Avreste potuto prendere un volo da Firenze per risparmiare tempo. Comunque **potreste** cominciare a Pisa, andare a vedere la Torre ... Poi Fleur **potrebbe** visitare i musei, mentre tu, Tony, **potresti** andare a vedere il Palio. Non so se riuscirai a trovare posto, ma **potresti** provare almeno. **Potrebbe** essere interessante anche fare una passeggiata lungo le mura antiche di Lucca. Poi da Lucca si **può** prendere il pullman per Firenze ... è più veloce del treno. Se **potete**, lasciate i bagagli alla stazione. Il centro di Firenze non è molto grande e si **può** girare anche a piedi. In una giornata **potete** vedere i principali monumenti: il Duomo, Palazzo Pitti, il Ponte Vecchio. Se poi avete tempo, **potete / potreste** visitare anche San Lorenzo e la Cappella dei Medici... Allora, Fleur **potrebbe** approfittare delle ore libere per fare degli acquisti. Ci sono bellissimi negozi. Se vuoi, Tony, **potresti** comprare qualcosa anche tu!

Unit 9

Exercise 1

Senta, scusi! Come arrivo alla Biblioteca Bodleiana? / Dunque...uscendo dal Museo, **giri** a destra, **vada** diritto per questa strada, che si chiama St Aldates, poi al semaforo **giri** a destra, questa è la High Street, **continui** per 200 metri, e dopo la Chiesa di St Mary the Virgin, **volti** a sinistra...... **attraversi** la piazza della Radcliffe Camera e l'entrata alla Biblioteca Bodleiana è proprio di fronte. / Ah, grazie. Lei è molto gentile.

Exercise 2

Free composition: these are only suggestions you might give your friend and his girlfriend.

Vai a vedere i chiostri di Santa Chiara. Cerca di visitare anche il Palazzo Reale e il Museo nazionale dove ci sono molti oggetti trovati a Pompei. Se la tua ragazza vuole comprare vestiti, andate al Vomero o a Via Toledo, dove ci sono dei negozi molto eleganti. Prendete la funicolare per arrivare al Vomero.

Assaggia le sfogliatelle e bevi un po' di limoncello. Per l'alloggio, prenota una camera al Majestic. Oppure, se preferisci, spendi meno e vai al Terminus, vicino alla stazione ferroviaria. Prova a visitare i posti interessanti anche fuori città, ad esempio, Capri. Prendi l'aliscafo per arrivarci. Oppure vai a Sorrento - prendi la Circumvesuviana, è un piccolo treno che parte da Piazza Garibaldi.

Unit 10

Exercise 1

Allora, questo è (mio fratello) Marco. Questa è (sua moglie) Marina, e questi sono (i loro figli) Carlotta e Simone. Questa, invece, è (mia sorella) Irma, con (suo marito) Ugo, e (le loro figlie) Flavia e Diana. (La loro) casa è vicino alla nostra. Ugo quindi è (mio cognato) e Flavia e Diana sono (le mie nipoti). E questo è (il loro cane) che dorme nella stanza di Flavia.

Exercise 2

1. mettermi. 2. Mi metto. 3. mi sono messo. 4. ti sei fatto. 5. mi sono rotto. 6. si è portato. 7. Si è mangiata. 8. Togliti.

Unit 11

Exercise 1

Gianna	... è andata? ... avete fatto.
Claudia	... è stata ... siamo andati ... abbiamo preso.
Gianna	... avete fatto.
Claudia	... ho fatto ... ha letto ... abbiamo visto ... . Abbiamo mangiato, cucinato e dormito.
Gianna	... Si sono divertiti?
Claudia	... si sono lamentati ... hanno potuto ... Hanno giocato ..., sono andati ... hanno aiutato.

Exercise 2

Claudia e suo marito Giovanni hanno passato le vacanze in campagna. Non hanno fatto niente di speciale ma si sono riposati. Claudia ha fatto delle lunghe passeggiate, suo marito ha letto molti libri, e hanno cucinato, mangiato e dormito. I ragazzi si sono lamentati. Si sono annoiati perché non hanno potuto guardare la televisione.

Exercise 3

(Free composition – this is just a suggestion)

Carissima Daniela

Abbiamo fatto una vacanza bellissima in Scozia. Ci siamo fermati prima a Glasgow, nell'albergo Royal Hotel, in pieno centro. Il giorno dopo siamo andati a Loch Lomond, un lago bellissimo circondato di montagne. Poi siamo andati sempre con il pullman a Fort William, più al nord. Lì abbiamo visto le montagne e le coste, certi colori stupendi e pochi turisti, per fortuna. Dopo due notti al Castle Hotel di Fort William, ci siamo trasferiti ad Aviemore, posto di villeggiatura invernale. Aviemore è stata la base per una gita a Loch Ness e ad Inverness. Grande delusione - non abbiamo visto il mostro di Loch Ness. Il giorno dopo siamo andati nel Perthshire dove abbiamo fatto una visita ad una distilleria dove fanno il whisky Famous Grouse (quello che beve tuo padre). Lo stesso giorno siamo andati al famoso campo di golf a St Andrews che è piaciuto molto a mio marito, appassionato di golf. L'ultima tappa è stata la più bella perché abbiamo passato due notti nella capitale, Edimburgo. Abbiamo visto il castello e il palazzo di Holyrood e abbiamo anche fatto un po' di shopping: maglie di cashmire e qualche kilt! Il viaggio in totale è costato quasi L800.000 a testa, più i voli, ma è valsa proprio la pena, dovresti andare anche tu!

Unit 12

Exercise 1

■ *Why my mother was angry*
Andavo ... ho incontrato ... andava ... ho deciso ... aspettava ... sono tornato ... ha fatto.

(All the examples of *passato prossimo* represent one event or action. **Andavo, andava** and **aspettava** are examples of an incomplete action.)

■ *My birthday*

… aveva promesso … c'ero mai stata. Avevamo già preso … aveva offerto … si è ammalata … abbiamo dovuto … . È stata.

(All the examples of *passato prossimo* represent one action or event. The *trapassato* (pluperfect) represents actions already completed – or not – before the main action takes place.)

Exercise 2

Conoscevo Gianni da solo 5 mesi quando **abbiamo deciso** che **volevamo** sposarci. Quando **abbiamo dato** la notizia alle nostre famiglie, tutti **sono rimasti** molto sorpresi. **Abbiamo ricevuto** tanti consigli e tante prediche. Perché **ci sposavamo** così presto? Perché non **volevamo** aspettare? Chi **poteva** immaginare che il matrimonio **poteva** provocare tante discussioni! Mio fratello **si era sposato** un anno prima senza tutte queste storie. Ma la situazione **era** diversa, in quanto lui **conosceva** la sua futura moglie da 10 anni. **Erano** stati studenti insieme al liceo. Alla fine **abbiamo preso** la decisione di fidanzarci ma di fissare la data del matrimonio per il 2000. Così tutti i nostri parenti **avrebbero avuto** tempo di abituarsi all'idea e di organizzare una bella festa.

Unit 13

Exercise 1

Sandra forse andrà in Spagna a lavorare quando sarà laureata. Luca forse andrà a lavorare con suo padre, che lo pagherà bene. Non dovrà lavorare troppo, e fra dieci anni forse avrà fatto i primi miliardi. Fra dieci anni Sandra forse avrà sposato uno spagnolo e avrà fatto tre figli.

Exercise 2

Where are you going on holiday next year? / We intend to go to the USA. Maybe we'll go and see some relatives. My husband doesn't want to go to Italy like we did this year. / You must be bored going to Italy by now, and always Calabria. You must have seen all of Calabria. / Well, not all, but maybe it'll be enough for now!

Exercise 3

1. Quando io **verrò** a cena, vi **porterò** un regalo. 2. Se tu **vedrai** Marco, digli che lo **chiamerò** fra alcuni giorni. 3. Appena i bambini **arriveranno** al mare, **faranno** un bagno. 4. Quando **farà** caldo, gli ospiti **avranno** sete

e **bisognerà** prendere delle bottiglie di acqua minerale. 5. Domani sera quando **finiranno** di lavorare, i miei zii **verranno** qui al mare. 6. Ad agosto quando io e mio marito **andremo** in Argentina, il figlio più piccolo **rimarrà** qui.

Unit 14

Exercise 1

1. vorrei. 2. vuoi. 3. vorrei. 4. volete. 5. vuole. 6. vorrei. 7. volete. 8. voglio. 9. Vogliamo. 10. vogliamo.

Exercise 2

Mia madre è molto difficile. Io ho 15 anni ma mi tratta come una bambina di 12 anni. Non **vuole** che io esca la sera con i miei amici, oppure mi fa uscire ma **vuole** che torni prima di mezzanotte. Io invece **vorrei** andare in discoteca con gli altri e rimanere fino alle 2.00. L'altro giorno **volevo** andare al cinema e ho chiesto dei soldi a mia madre, ma lei non **voleva** che io andassi al cinema da sola. Non **ha voluto** darmi i soldi. **Vorrebbe** che io rimanessi a casa con lei.

Unit 15

Exercise 1

Si ascolteranno ... si visitano ... si va ... essere comprati. ... va incluso ... verrà riservata.

Exercise 2

In Italia **si mangia** molta pasta. La pasta **viene mangiata** all'ora di pranzo, soprattutto al centro e al sud del paese. Al nord, invece, **si mangiano** più spesso il riso e la polenta. La pasta **è servita** con sugo di pomodoro o di carne. **Va servita** al dente, e quindi non troppo cotta. A Bologna le tagliatelle vengono servite spesso con prosciutto e panna mentre in Sicilia gli spaghetti vengono serviti con melanzane.

Unit 16

Exercise 1

Ti **piace** andare al cinema? / Sì, mi **piace** molto. E a te? / Sì, anche **a me** piace. / Che tipi di film ti **piacciono**? / **A me piacciono** i film romantici ma a mio marito non **piacciono** i film di questo genere. / E **a lui** che tipi di film **piacciono**? / Nessuno.

Exercise 2

1. Gli piace il pane con la marmellata. 2. Le piace l'insalata verde. 3. Ci piacciono le patate fritte. 4. Gli piacciono gli hamburgers. 5. Le piacciono le patate. 6. Gli piace la pasta. 7. Gli piace la carne. 8. Mi piace la pizza / mi piacciono i gelati.

Unit 17

Exercise 1

1. Io penso che **bastino** … 2. Credo che la scuola **sia** … 3. Mi sembra che la scuola **stia** … 4. Penso che la scuola **abbia** … 5. Credo che gli insegnanti **abbiano** … 6. Mi sembra che i ragazzi **possano** … 7. Credo che i ragazzi **debbano** … 8. Penso che la scuola **organizzi** … 9. Mi pare che i pasti **siano** … 10. Mi sembra che i ragazzi **abbiano** … 11. Penso che ci **sia** …

Exercise 2

1. Mia madre **pensa che io vada a letto** prima di mezzanotte. 2. Mia madre **crede che io studi**. 3. Mia madre **pensa che io abbia preso** un bel voto. 4. Mia madre **crede che io sia stata promossa** in tutte le materie. 5. Mia madre **pensa che** la sera **io stia** a casa della mia amica. 6. Mia madre **crede che non esca** con nessuno. 7. Mia madre **pensa che** i miei amici **siano ragazzi seri**. 8. Mia madre **crede che io vada** in autobus. 9. Mia madre **pensa che io non mangi** mai cose di questo tipo. 10. Mia madre **crede che io non beva** mai alcolici.

Unit 18

Exercise 1

Viaggiatore	Bisogna che io sia … devo prendere?
Impiegato	… deve … bisogna che prenda … deve pagare.
Impiegato	Vuole.

Exercises 2 and 3 are free choice.

Exercise 4
(Free choice: this is just a suggestion)

Cara Chiara
Non c' è bisogno che voi mandiate bigliettini. Dovete invece avvertire gli amici e i parenti stretti telefonicamente. Se però avete molti parenti e amici in altre città, bisogna che comunichiate la notizia per posta. In questo caso è essenziale far stampare dei bigliettini. Bisogna mandarli dopo la nascita, quando rientrerai a casa dall'ospedale. Sul cartoncino, bisogna che mettiate tutti i nomi del bambino, se non sono più di tre. I confetti, invece, bisogna darli solamente in occasione del battesimo. Bisogna che questi siano celesti per un maschietto e rosa per una femminuccia.

Unit 19

Exercise 1

vengano ... vengano ... migliori ... sia stato varato ... faccia ... sia risolto.

Holidays, a time when animals are abandoned. Every summer it is estimated that over 25,000 dogs and thousands of other pets are left to die. 'In the Valtellina,' explains Anna Tosi, a voluntary worker at the 'Enpa' kennels, 'we receive hundreds of requests from people who want their dogs to be looked after in our Centre.' Unless the situation improves, the stray dog problem will become a danger both to man and livestock. Any measures taken up to now have not achieved encouraging results. 'It is to be hoped that the new law just approved', adds the socialist M.P. Dino Mazza, 'will get the Italians to kick their habit of putting a dog under the tree at Christmas and out on the motorway in August.' But it is unlikely that this problem will be solved easily.

Exercise 2

Luciana ... partano ... salutino.
Chiara ... abbiano trovato ... siano.

Exercise 3

1. **Sono contenta** che la Scozia **abbia** vinto la partita e che **giochi** contro l'Italia stasera. 2. **Mi dispiace** che ci **sia** sciopero. Ma **sono contenta** che non ci **siano** lezioni. 3. **Mi dispiace** che tua madre **sia caduta** e che **si sia** rotta il braccio. 4. **Mi dispiace / sono desolata** che il tuo cane **sia** stato investito da una macchina. 5. **Non sono stupita** che l'insegnante **bocci**

Giovanni all'esame di storia contemporanea. 6. **Sono contenta** che stasera tua zia **prepari** la pasta con le vongole. 7. **Mi dispiace** che tuo fratello ti **abbia** preso in prestito il CD nuovo e l'**abbia** graffiato. 8. **Sono stupita** che **venga** anche la tua ex-ragazza stasera. 9. **Sono contenta** che i tuoi genitori ti **diano** L100.000 per il tuo compleanno. 10. **Sono contento** che tuo padre ti **offra** un viaggio a Parigi per festeggiare l'onomastico. 11. **Mi stupisce** che Gianna **debba** stare a dieta. 12. **Mi dispiace** che fra te e il calcio, il tuo ragazzo **preferisca** il calcio.

Unit 20

Exercise 1

1. Le dispiacerebbe spostare il piede? 2. Le dispiacerebbe aprire la finestra? 3. Le dispiacerebbe chiudere la porta? 4. Le dispiacerebbe passarmi lo zucchero? (Potrebbe passarmi lo zucchero?) 5. Le dispiacerebbe prestarmi la penna? (Mi potrebbe prestare la penna?) 6. Mi potrebbe dire l'ora? 7. Mi potresti prestare L20.000? 8. Mi potresti dare una mano?

Exercise 2

penso … si svegliasse … risistemasse … immaginare … avessimo dormito … era bellissimo … facesse.

It was strange what happened when I slept in my grandmother's bed…when I woke up, I found myself in exactly the same position… I think that my grandmother woke up a good bit before me and put me back in the same position, but it was nice to imagine that we had slept in that position for the whole night. Anyway, it was really nice that she did everything possible to make me believe it.

Exercise 3

Ogni tanto andavo a casa di Bruno ed era facile che **restassimo** fino alle due di notte a chiacchierare, perché era l'unica persona con cui io **potessi** parlare liberamente. Lui voleva che io gli **parlassi** in inglese, perché stava studiando la lingua, ma io non mi sentivo più a mio agio nonostante **fosse** la mia madre lingua. Mia madre non sapeva né mi chiedeva mai con chi **uscissi** e lasciava che io **prendessi** la macchina senza farmi domande di nessun tipo.

Unit 21

Exercise 1

Andrea   ... pensavo ... fossi già partito.

Nando   ... è impossibile ... l'abbia controllata ... non l'avessimo mai portata.

Nando   ... sapevamo se fosse ... benché avesse fatto ... senza che dovessimo.

Andrea   Era meglio ... aveste aspettato!

Exercise 2

La vita è piena di sbagli. Noi avevamo prenotato l'albergo a Venezia su consiglio di un'amica. Non **sapevamo** che lei non *fosse mai stata* a Venezia, e che il nome dell'albergo *l'avesse trovato* su una vecchia guida turistica. Sarà stato bello cinquanta anni fa, ma non più. E il ristorante poi....! Morivamo di sete! **Nonostante** *avessimo* detto al cameriere tre volte di portare del vino rosso, **ha portato** solo acqua minerale. **Peccato** poi che il cuoco *abbia dimenticato* di togliere lo spago prima di servire l'arrosto... **mi chiedevo** poi **perché** mio marito *avesse deciso* di mangiarlo, ma lui, poveretto, **aveva pensato** che il cuoco *avesse preparato* una specialità tipica e che lo spago ne *fosse* una parte essenziale. **Avremmo mangiato** meglio alla mensa degli studenti – e **avremmo** anche speso di meno.

Life is full of mistakes. We had booked the hotel in Venice on the advice of a friend. We didn't know that she had never been to Venice, but had found the name in an old guide book. It might have been nice 50 years ago but no longer. And the restaurant ...! We were dying of thirst. Despite the fact that we had asked the waiter three times to bring us some red wine, he brought only mineral water. A pity too that the chef forgot to take off the string around the roast before serving it. I wondered why my husband had decided to eat it, but he, poor thing, had thought the chef prepared some typical local speciality and that the string was an essential part of it. We would have eaten better at the student canteen, and we would have spent less too.

Unit 22

Exercise 1

Carla   Ciao, Maria. Come mai non sei venuta stasera?

Maria   **Sarei venuta** se non avessi avuto tante altre cose da fare.

Carla   Peccato. Se tu **fossi venuta,** ti avrei fatto conoscere mio cugino.

Maria   Pazienza! Sarà per la prossima volta. Se lui **viene** per Natale,
          fammi sapere.

Carla   Non mancherò. Intanto se tu non **fossi** sempre così impegnata,
          ti inviterei a cena.

Maria   Se mi **inviti**, accetto volentieri!

Exercise 2

(Free composition: these are only suggestions)
1. … mangeremmo meglio. 2. … potrei uscire tutte le sere/potrei fare
quello che voglio. 3. … avrei una camera tutta mia. 4. … ci vedremmo
più spesso / ci potremmo vedere più facilmente. 5. … non mangerebbe la
carne.

Exercise 3

(Free composition: these are only suggestions)
1. … sarei rimasta in Italia / avrei parlato italiano meglio / avrei avuto una
vita più felice. 2. saremmo più bravi/avremmo avuto un voto migliore.
3. … ti saresti divertita / avresti trovato un lavoro migliore. 4. … avrebbe
conosciuto l'uomo dei suoi sogni. 5. … non sarebbe andato a finire contro
un muro / non avrebbe distrutto la macchina.

GRAMMAR APPENDIX

This section of the book covers only points that have not been covered in the units, or have been mentioned only in passing. It includes a list of irregular verbs and a list of verb links, for easy reference (13.2 and 13.3).

1 Nouns with irregular plurals

Nouns with regular plurals are illustrated in unit 2. Here we show only those nouns which do not follow those patterns.

1.1 Invariable plural forms

(nouns with the same form in both singular and plural)

Nouns ending in *-i*

These are mainly feminine:

la crisi	*crisis*	le crisi	*crises*

But note:

il brindisi	*toast*	i brindisi	*toasts*
(e.g. to bride and groom)			

Feminine nouns ending in *-ie*

la serie	*series*	le serie	*series*

But note:

la moglie	*wife*	le mogli	*wives*

Abbreviated words

la bici(cletta)	*bike*	le bici	*bikes*
il cinema(tografo)	*cinema*	i cinema	*cinemas*

Words borrowed from other languages (mainly ending in a consonant)

il night	*nightclub*	i night	*nightclubs*
il computer	*computer*	i computer	*computers*

1.2 Irregular and other plural forms

Nouns with masculine singular ending in -*o*, but feminine plural ending in -*a*

il paio	*pair*	le paia	*pairs*
l'uovo	*egg*	le uova	*eggs*
il migliaio	*thousand*	le migliaia	*thousands*

Nouns with masculine singular ending in -*o*, and alternative plurals (masculine ending in -*i*, feminine ending in -*a*)

These nouns have a regular masculine plural ending in **-i** and an irregular feminine plural ending in **-a**. Often the regular plural has a figurative meaning, while the irregular plural has a literal meaning:

il braccio	*arm*	le braccia	*arms (of a person)*
		i bracci	*arms (e.g. of a chandelier)*

But in some cases there is no difference in meaning:

il lenzuolo	*sheet*	le lenzuola	*sheets*
		i lenzuoli	*sheets*

Masculine nouns ending in -*co*, -*go*

Nouns where the stress falls on the second last syllable form their plural in **-chi** or **-ghi**, keeping the hard 'g' sound:

il luogo	*place*	i luoghi	*places*
il fico	*fig*	i fichi	*figs*

Unfortunately there are many exceptions:

l'amico	*friend*	gli amici	*friends*

Words where the stress generally falls *before* the second last syllable, form their plural in **-ci** and **-gi** with a soft 'g':

l'asparago	*asparagus*	gli asparagi	*asparagus*
il medico	*doctor*	i medici	*doctors*

But again there are very many exceptions:

| il catalogo | *catalogues* | i cataloghi | *catalogues* |

Feminine nouns ending in -ca, -ga

These form plural in **-che** and **-ghe**:

| l'amica | *friend* | le amiche | *friends* |

Feminine nouns ending in -cia, -gia

These have a plural ending **-cie** or **-gie** if there is a vowel before the **-cia**, or **-gia**:

| la farmacia | *chemist's* | le farmacie | *chemists* |
| la valigia | *suitcase* | le valigie | *suitcases* |

They have plural ending **-ce** or **-ge** if there is a consonant before the **-cia** or **-gia**:

| la spiaggia | *beach* | le spiagge | *beaches* |
| la mancia | *tip* | le mance | *tips* |

Masculine nouns ending in -io

If the stress falls on the **i**, the **i** is doubled:

| lo zio | *uncle* | gli zii | *uncles* |

Otherwise it does not:

| lo studio | *study* | gli studi | *studies* |

Compound nouns

Nouns made up of two different words stuck together sometimes have rather unusual plural forms:

| il capostazione | *station master* | i capistazione | *station masters* |
| il fuoribordo | *motor boat* | i fuoribordo | *motor boats* |

Since the rules – and the exceptions – are numerous, it is safer to use a good dictionary to check the plural of such nouns.

2 Adjectives

2.1 *bello, buono, grande, santo*

All the adjectives listed above can take different forms when found before a noun.

bello

Bello has the same forms as the definite article **il, lo, la,** etc:

un **bel** ragazzo	*a nice-looking boy*
una **bella** casa in campagna	*a beautiful house in the country*
un **bello** specchio antico	*a beautiful antique mirror*

Hanno ricevuto dei **bei** regali	*They received some lovely presents.*
Hai fatto delle **belle** foto.	*You've taken some lovely photos.*
... una casa con dei **begli** alberi intorno.	*... a house with beautiful trees around*

buono

In the singular **buono** has the same forms as the indefinite article **un, uno, una,** etc:

un **buon** ristorante	*a good restaurant*
un **buono** studente	*a good student*
una **buona** persona	*a good person*
una **buon**'idea	*a good idea*

grande

Before masculine singular nouns **grande** can have a shortened form but this is optional:

un **grande** capitano / un **gran** capitano   *a great captain*

Do not use the shortened form if the noun starts with a vowel or with **gn, ps, s, x, z**:

un **grande** albergo	*a great hotel*
un **grande** scultore	*a great sculptor*

santo

Finally, **santo** (feminine **santa**) meaning *holy, saint* can have a shortened form before a masculine singular name, unless it begins with **gn, ps, s, x, z**:

San Marco
Santo Stefano
Santa Lucia

And can drop the final **-o / -a** vowel before a name beginning with a vowel:

Sant'Ambrogio
Sant'Anna

3 Comparison

3.1 Comparative adjectives

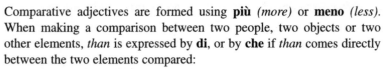

Più, meno

Comparative adjectives are formed using **più** *(more)* or **meno** *(less)*. When making a comparison between two people, two objects or two other elements, *than* is expressed by **di**, or by **che** if *than* comes directly between the two elements compared:

Lui è meno bravo **di** te.   *He is less clever than you.*
Marco è più simpatico **di** Giuliano. *Marco is nicer than Giuliano.*
Fa meno freddo oggi **che** ieri. *It is less cold today than yesterday.*
Adesso si mangia più pesce   *Nowadays one eats more fish*
che carne.   *than meat.*

Di *(than)* can combine with **il, lo, la**, etc:

Gli italiani sono più simpatici *The Italians are nicer than the*
  degli inglesi.   *English.*

Buono – più buono – migliore

Buono *(good)* has two comparative forms: **più buono** and **migliore**. There is little difference in meaning but in a more general context **migliore** is normally used.

I gelati francesi sono **buoni**, ma i *French ice-creams are good, but*
  gelati italiani sono **più buoni**. *Italian ice-creams are better.*
Con l'antenna parabolica, la qualità *With a satellite dish, the quality*
  della trasmissione è **migliore**. *of transmission is better.*

cattivo – più cattivo – peggiore

Cattivo *(bad)* has two comparative forms: **più cattivo** and **peggiore**. There is little difference in meaning but **peggiore** is normally used in a more general context.

Questo vino è **cattivo**, ma l'altro *This wine is bad, but the other*
  è ancora **più cattivo**.   *is even worse.*
Questa pensione **non** è **buona**, *This hotel isn't good but the*
  ma l'altra è **peggiore**.   *other is worse.*

grande – più grande – maggiore

While **più grande** can be used to refer either to physical size or age difference, **maggiore** generally refers to age difference or to an abstract quality, but not to physical size:

Milano è **più grande** di Torino.	*Milan is bigger than Turin.*
La mia sorella **maggiore** (or **più grande**) si chiama Rosa.	*My older sister is called Rosa.*
Per gli studenti, lo sport è un tema di **maggiore** interesse.	*For the students, sport is a topic of greater interest.*

piccolo – più piccolo – minore

While **più piccolo** can be used to refer either to physical size or age difference, **minore** generally refers to age difference or to an abstract quality, rather than physical size:

La nostra camera è **più piccola** della vostra.	*Our room is smaller than yours.*
Il suo fratello **minore** si chiamava Luca.	*His younger brother was called Luca.*
Questo episodio è di **minore** importanza.	*This incident is of lesser importance.*

Plural forms

Both **maggiore** and **minore** have plural forms: **maggiori**, **minori**.

3.2 Relationship of equality: adjectives

tanto ... quanto; così ... come

To compare two things of equal qualities, use **tanto ... quanto** or **così ... come**. In each case the second element can be omitted, without changing the meaning.

Una pensione può essere **tanto** comoda **quanto** l'albergo di lusso.	*A guest house can be just as comfortable as a luxury hotel.*

Così and **tanto** can be omitted from the sentence, without changing the meaning.

3.3 Superlative adjectives

While **più** and **meno** are used to express *more* and *less* respectively, *most, least* are expressed using **il più** and **il meno** with the adjective:

È **il** ristorante **meno caro** della città.	*It's the least expensive restaurant in town.*
È **la** chiesa **più** bella di Venezia.	*It's the most beautiful church in Venice.*

The common adjectives sometimes come before the noun:

È **il più** bel ragazzo della classe.   *He's the best-looking boy in the class.*

buono, cattivo, grande, piccolo

Buono, cattivo, grande, piccolo all have two different forms of superlative each with slightly different meanings *(see comparative forms above)*:

Gli incidenti stradali sono **la maggiore** causa di morte in Italia.	*Road accidents are the biggest (greatest) cause of death in Italy.*
La FIAT 500 è **la** macchina **più piccola** di tutte.	*The 500 is the smallest car of all. (physical size)*

Superlative with no comparison implied

To express a superlative quality, when no comparison is being made, use **molto** o **estremamente** o **veramente** with the adjective:

I bambini erano **veramente** stanchi.	*The kids were really tired.*

Or add the suffix **-issimo** onto the end:

Questi fiori sono **bellissimi**.	*These flowers are very beautiful.*

And for the four adjectives mentioned above, there are alternative superlative forms **ottimo, pessimo, massimo** and **minimo**:

Ottimo il dolce! Chi l'ha fatto?	*Fantastic this cake! Who made it?*
È **pessimo** questo tema.	*This essay is rubbish.*
È il **massimo**!	*That's really the best yet! (often used ironically)*
Non ha fatto il **minimo** sforzo.	*He didn't make the slightest effort.*

3.4 Comparative adverbs

più, meno

As for adjectives, comparisons can be made using **più** *(more)* and **meno** *(less)* along with the appropriate adverb:

Gianfranco cammina **più** velocemente di me.	*Gianfranco walks faster than me.*
Gianfranco cammina **meno** velocemente di Filippo.	*Gianfranco walks less quickly than Filippo.*

bene, male, molto, poco

These four adverbs have irregular comparative forms **meglio**, **peggio**, **più**, **meno**, respectively:

Giuliana guida **bene**, ma Mariangela guida **meglio**.	*Giuliana drives well, but Mariangela drives better.*
Franco cucina **male**, ma Giovanni cucina **peggio**.	*Franco cooks badly, but Giovanni cooks worse.*
Più imparo questa lingua, **più** difficile la trovo.	*The more I study this language the more difficult I find it.*
Marco studia **molto**, ma Monica studia **di più**.	*Marco studies a lot, but Monica studies more.*
Meno lavoro fai, **meno** guadagni.	*The less work you do the less you earn.*
Arabella lavora **poco**, ma Marina lavora **di meno**.	*Arabella works little, but Marina works less.*

3.5 Relationship of equality: adverbs

tanto...quanto; così....come

We have already seen these pairs used with adjectives. Their use with adverbs is similar. The first element of each pair can be omitted:

Sandra guida **così** male **come** sua sorella.	*Sandra drives just as badly as her sister.*

3.6 Superlative adverbs

il più possibile / molto / -issimamente

There are several ways to express superlative adverbs. Sometimes no comparison is implied. Study these examples:

Guidava **molto lentamente**.	*He drove very slowly.*
Guidava **lentissimamente**.	*He drove very slowly.*
Guidava **il più lentamente possibile**.	*He drove very slowly / as slowly as possible.*
Guidava **il più lentamente di tutti**.	*He drove the slowest of everyone.*

and

Lo vedo **il meno possibile**.	*I see him as little as possible.*

bene, male, molto, poco

These adverbs have a normal superlative form ending in **-issimo**:

Ha sciato **benissimo**.	*She skied very well.*
L'ha fatto **malissimo**.	*He did it very badly.*
Ho mangiato **moltissimo**.	*I've eaten loads.*
Hai studiato **pochissimo**.	*You've studied very little.*

Their irregular superlative forms **il meglio, il peggio, il più, il meno** respectively can also be used as a relative superlative (i.e. comparing with one's own or others' efforts):

Ha fatto **il meglio** possibile.	*He did as best he could.*
Ha studiato **il più** possibile.	*He studied as much as possible.*
Cerca di camminare **il meno** possibile.	*Try to walk as little as possible.*

The forms **il meglio, il peggio** can also be used as nouns (*the best, the worst*):

Ha dato **il meglio** di sé stesso.	*She gave the best of herself.*
Non sai ancora **il peggio**.	*You don't know the worst.*

4 Pronouns

There are several types of pronouns. The most important group is that of personal pronouns, including direct object, indirect object, subject pronouns and stressed pronouns. The direct object pronouns are illustrated in units 4 and 14. Here we explain other types of pronouns.

4.1 Indirect object pronouns

The forms **mi, ti, gli, le Le, ci, vi, gli/loro** are used with any verb that takes an *indirect* object:

Verbs of *giving, lending*, etc. such as **dare, prestare, portare**:

| **Vi** porto il conto? | *Shall I bring (to) you the bill?* |
| **Ti** ha dato il resto? | *Did he give (to) you the change?* |

Or expressing the idea of doing something for someone:

| **Mi** compreresti il giornale? | *Would you buy the newspaper for me?* |
| **Ti** preparo un caffè? | *Shall I make (for) you a coffee?* |

4.2 Combined object pronouns

Look what happens when direct object **mi, ti, lo, la**, etc. (see unit 14) meets indirect object **mi, ti, gli, le** etc. The indirect object pronouns come first and change form slightly. **Mi, ti, ci, vi** become **me, te, ce, ve** when before a direct object pronoun, to produce **me lo, te lo** etc. **Gli, le, Le** combine with the direct object pronouns to form a single word **glielo** (etc.).

Indirect	*Direct*	*Combined*
mi	lo	me lo
ti	lo	te lo
gli	lo	glielo
le	lo	glielo
Le	lo	glielo
ci	lo	ce lo
vi	lo	ve lo
gli	lo	glielo

The pattern is the same whether the direct object pronoun is **lo, la, li** or **le** (for example me **li**, me **le** etc.). The exception to the pattern is **loro** which comes after the verb and does not combine with the other pronouns.

Use of combined pronouns

Here are examples of how they are used:

| Come si apre questa bottiglia? | *How does one open this bottle?* |
| **Te la** apro io. | *I'll open it for you.* |

I ragazzi hanno lasciato questo libro. *The kids have left behind this book.*
Glielo mandiamo per posta.   *We'll mail it to them.*

Glielo can mean *it to him* or *it to her* or *it to them*. To avoid any confusion or ambiguity, you can use **a lui, a lei, a loro**:

Lo mando **a lui**.   *I send it to him.*
Lo mando **a lei**.   *I send it to her.*
Lo mando **a loro**.   *I send it to them.*

4.3 Position of pronouns

Normally the pronouns come *before* the verb, but this is not true in all cases:

After the infinitive

The pronouns come after and are joined onto the end of the infinitive (the **-are, -ere, -ire** form):

Sono andata in centro per   *I went to the centre to buy it.*
  comprarla.
Ho deciso di **spedirgli** una cartolina. *I've decided to send him a postcard.*
Mi ha telefonato per **chiedermelo**. *He rang me to ask me for it.*

With the auxiliary verbs *volere, dovere, sapere, potere, preferire*

With these auxiliary verbs, the object pronouns can either be joined to the end of the infinitive, as above, or come before both verbs:

Lo puoi comprare al centro.   *You can buy it in town.*
or Puoi comprar**lo** al centro.

Voglio parlar**gli** chiaro.   *I want to speak clearly to him.*
or **Gli** voglio parlare chiaro.

Deve dir**glielo** appena possibile. *She must tell him it as soon as possible.*
or **Glielo** deve dire appena possibile.

With the gerund *(-ando,-endo form)*

The object pronouns are joined to the end of the gerund:

Telefonando**ti** di sera, risparmio *By phoning you in the evening,*
  parecchio.   *I save a lot.*

Riparando**telo** gratis, ti faccio un grande favore.	*Repairing it for you free, I'm doing you a big favour.*

With **stare** and the gerund, the object pronouns can be joined to the end of the gerund, as above, *or* can come before **stare**:

Lo stavo guardando ora.	*I was just looking at it now.*
or Stavo guardando**lo** ora.	

With the *tu, noi, voi* imperative (order) forms

The object pronouns are joined to the end of these imperative (order) forms:

Chiamiamo**li**!	*Let's call them!*
Telefona**gli**!	*Ring him !*
Passateme**lo**!	*Pass it to me!*

The same applies to reflexive pronouns:

Alza**ti**!	*Get up!*

When attached to the one-syllable **tu** imperative forms such as **da' ! fa'! di'! sta'! va'!** the initial consonant of the pronoun doubles:

Da**llo** a tuo fratello!	*Give it to your brother!*
Da**mmelo**!	*Give it to me!*
Di**mmi** cosa vuoi!	*Tell me what you want!*
Fa**cci** un piacere!	*Do us a favour!*
Va**ttene**!	*Go away!*
Fa**mmi** un piacere!	*Do me a favour!*

But not in the case of **gli**:

Di**gli** di andare via!	*Tell him to go away!*
Da**gli** una mano.	*Give him a hand.*

With negative imperative forms

With the negative imperative forms for **tu, noi** and **voi**, the pronoun has two possible positions:

Non segui**rmi**!	*Don't follow me!*
or Non **mi** seguire!	
Non compriamo**lo**!	*Let's not buy it!*
or Non **lo** compriamo!	

| Non mangiate**li**! | *Don't eat them!* |
| *or* Non **li** mangiate! | |

| Non alzate**vi**! | *Don't get up!* |
| *or* Non **vi** alzate! | |

With the *Lei* (formal) imperative form

With the **Lei** imperative form, the object pronouns always go before:

| **Lo** prenda pure! | *Please take it!* |
| Non **lo** prenda! | *Don't take it!* |

4.4 *ci*

Ci is generally treated in the same way as the object pronouns and is often found with them. It has two main functions: firstly, as a particle meaning *there* or *to there*. It's occasionally replaced by **vi** but this is far less common in spoken Italian. Secondly, it acts as a pronoun, replacing **a** and a noun.

Mi piace Londra; **ci** abito da	*I like London; I've lived there*
sei anni.	*for six years.*
Andando**ci** di lunedì, troverete	*Going there on a Monday, you*
meno gente.	*will find less people.*
Ti ci porto io, se vuoi.	*I'll take you there if you want.*

Ci can be used with a verb which takes **a**, such as **credere, riuscire, pensare**:

| Credi a quello che dice? | *Do you believe what he says?* |
| No, non **ci** credo. | *No, I don't believe it.* |

Or with a verb which normally takes **con**:

| Hai parlato con il direttore? | *Did you speak to the director?* |
| Sì, **ci** ho parlato ieri. | *Yes, I spoke to him yesterday.* |

Ci is also used in phrases where the verb **avere** is combined with direct object pronouns **lo, la, li, le**. **Lo, la** are often abbreviated before **avere** to **l'**. But the plurals **li** and **le** should not be abbreviated.

| Hai il giornale? No, non **ce l'**ho. | *Do you have the newspaper?* |
| | *No, I don't have it.* |

It is also used in the idiomatic expression **farcela** (*to manage it, to cope*):

Ce la fai a finire quella relazione? *Can you manage to finish that report?*

And with the verbs **vedere, sentire** where it has a non-specific meaning:

Non **ci** vedo.	*I can't see anything.*
Ci senti, Chiara?	*Can you hear, Chiara?*

4.5 *ne*

Ne is a pronoun meaning *of it, of them* and used replacing **di** and an object or person:

Quanti figli hai?	*How many children do you have?*
Ne ho tre.	*I have three (of them).*
Quanto pane vuole?	*How much bread do you want?*
Ne prendo un chilo, grazie.	*I'll have a kilo, thanks.*

When there are other object pronouns, **ne** comes after them:

Me **ne** dai un po'?   *Will you give me a bit (of it)?*

When **ne** is used with a past tense and followed by a number or quantity, the past participle has to agree:

Hai visto dei gabbiani?	*Have you seen any seagulls?*
Sì, **ne** ho visti tre.	*Yes, I have seen three.*

When no quantity is mentioned, **ne** means *some* or *any*:

Vuoi delle patatine?	*Do you want some crisps?*
No, grazie. **Ne** ho.	*No, thanks. I have some.*
or Sì, grazie. Non **ne** ho.	*Yes, please. I haven't got any.*

Ne can be used meaning *of it* replacing **di** and an object:

Agostino non ti parla mai **della faccenda**?	*Does Agostino ever speak to you about the affair?*
Sì, **ne** parla spesso.	*Yes, he often speaks of it.*

It can also be used when the reference is to **da**:

Sono usciti **dal ristorante**?	*Have they come out of the restaurant?*
Ne escono adesso.	*They're coming out of it just now.*

Ne is used in certain idiomatic expressions:

Me **ne** vado.	*I'm going away.*
Non **ne** posso più.	*I can't take any more.*
Ne va della mia reputazione.	*My reputation is at stake.*

4.6 Direct object pronouns with *passato prossimo*

The participle (**mangiato, capito**, etc.) has to agree with a direct object pronoun:

Hai visto i bambini?	*Have you seen the children?*
No, non **li** ho vist**i**.	*No, I haven't seen them.*
Avevi già conosciuto Lidia?	*Had you already met Lidia?*
No, non **l'**avevo mai vist**a** prima.	*No, I had never seen her before.*
Mario avrà già studiato i verbi?	*Will Marco already have studied the verbs?*
Sì, **li** avrà già studiat**i**.	*Yes, he'll have studied them already.*

5 Indefinites

5.1 *Alcun, ogni, ognuno, ciascuno, tale, altro*

For the use of **qualche** and the plural forms of **alcuni, alcune** meaning *some*, see unit 3.

alcun (some, any...)

The singular forms **alcun, alcuno, alcuna, alcun'** are used only after a negative, with the meaning *any*. They have the same endings as **un/uno** etc.

Non ho **alcun'**idea.	*I haven't a clue.*
Non c'era **alcuna** ragione.	*There was no reason at all.*

ogni (every, each)

This is always singular, meaning *each, every*, and can refer to objects or people.

Ogni cosa è possibile.	*Everything is possible.*
Ogni ospite paga lo stesso.	*Each guest pays the same.*

ognuno (each one, everyone)

Like **ogni**, this can only be singular and means *each one, everyone*.

Ognuno fa quello che vuole.	*Each does what he wants.*

ciascun, ciascuno (each, each one)

This is singular only. As an adjective, it means *each* and as a pronoun means *each one*. As an adjective, it has the same endings as the indefinite article **un**: **ciascun, ciascuno, ciascuna, ciascun'**:

Ci sono quattro persone a **ciascun** tavolo.	*There are four people at each table.*

Used on its own, it has just two forms: **ciascuno** and **ciascuna**:

Ciascuno dei bambini ha una camera separata.	*Each one of the children has a separate room.*

tale, un tale (such, somebody or other)

Tale has both singular and plural forms (**tale, tali**).

Used with a noun, it means *such*:

Ha un **tale** complesso che non riesce neanche a parlare.	*She has such a complex that she can't even speak.*

Used on its own, it means *somebody or other, 'some bloke', 'some guy'*:

Ho visto **un tale** che vendeva delle magliette.	*I saw some guy selling t-shirts.*

altro (another, other)

Altro as an adjective means *other, another* and as a pronoun means *anyone else, anything/something else*:

C'è un **altro** modello?	*Is there another style?*
Vuole **altro**?	*Do you want anything else?*
L'**altro** mio amico si chiama Marco.	*My other friend is called Marco.*
Un altro si sarebbe comportato diversamente.	*Someone else would have behaved differently.*

5.2 *qualunque, qualsiasi, chiunque*

This group of indefinites includes pronouns and adjectives meaning *-ever*, for example *whatever, whichever, whoever*:

qualunque, qualsiasi (any, whatever, any kind of...)

The meaning of these two indefinites varies according to their position:

Used *before* the noun, meaning *any, whatever*, these can only be used with a singular noun:

Farebbe **qualunque** cosa pur di vederla.	*He would do anything just to see her.*
Pagherebbe **qualsiasi** prezzo pur di avere quella macchina.	*He would pay any price just to have that car.*

Used *after* the noun, **qualunque** and **qualsiasi** can be used with a singular or plural noun, meaning *any kind of / any whatever / any old*:

Mettiti un vestito **qualunque**.	*Put on any old dress.*
Vanno bene dei panini **qualsiasi**.	*Any sandwiches will do.*

chiunque (anyone, whoever)

This has only a singular form and meaning. When meaning *whoever*, as in the second example, it is followed by the subjunctive verb form:

Chiunque può venire.	*Anyone can come.*
Chiunque sia, non è molto intelligente.	*Whoever he is, he's not very intelligent.*

6 Quantity

molto, troppo, poco, tutto, tanto, parecchio

All these have a characteristic in common. Used as an *adjective*, they have to agree with the noun they are describing. Used as a *noun* or *adverb*, their ending does not change:

molto (much, many, a lot)

Ci sono **molte** cose da vedere.	*There are lots of things to see.*
Ho mangiato **molto**.	*I've eaten a lot.*
Scrive **molto** bene.	*He writes very well.*

troppo (too much, too many)

Ieri c'erano **troppe** persone.	*Yesterday there were too many people.*
Ho mangiato **troppo**.	*I have eaten too much.*
È **troppo** giovane per andare al pub.	*He's too young to go to the pub.*

poco (little, few)

Ci sono **poche** cartoline.	*There are only a few postcards.*

Hai dormito **poco**.   *You haven't slept much.*
Sono un **poco** stanco.   *I am a bit tired.*

Poco is often abbreviated to **un po'**.

tutto (all of, everything)

I ragazzi hanno mangiato   *The boys have eaten all the pizza.*
tutta la pizza.
Prendi **tutto**!   *Take everything!*
Va **tutto** bene per domani sera.   *It's all fine for tomorrow evening.*

tanto (so much, so many; much, many)

Tanti studenti non controllano   *(So) many students never check*
mai la posta elettronica.   *their e-mail.*
Mi sento male, ho mangiato **tanto**. *I feel ill, I've eaten so much.*
È **tanto** gentile con me.   *She's so kind with me.*

parecchio (much, many)

Parecchi studenti non sanno   *Lots of students don't know where*
ancora dov'è la biblioteca.   *the library is yet.*
Ha girato **parecchio** in Italia.   *She's travelled a lot in Italy.*

7 Relative pronouns

che, cui, il quale

che (who, what)

La signora **che** lavora nell'ufficio   *The lady who works in the Tourist*
turistico è di Milano.   *Office is from Milan.*

Il treno **che** parte alle 10.00 arriva *The train which leaves at 10.00*
all'una.   *arrives at 1 o'clock.*

cui (who/whom, what)

With a preposition (**con, su, in, per, di, da, a**, etc.) **che** is replaced by **cui**:

L'amico **a cui** volevo telefonare   *The friend (to whom) I wanted*
è fuori.   *to telephone is out.*
La ragione **per cui** voglio andare   *The reason why I want to go*
a casa è semplice.   *home is simple.*

il quale (who/whom, what)

Both **che** and **cui** can be replaced by **il quale, la quale, i quali, le quali**, whose form reflects the gender and number of the person or object referred to:

Il canotto **con il quale** giocano i bambini è nostro.	*The rubber dinghy the children are playing with is ours.*

Adding a preposition (**a, di, da, in, su**) produces forms such as **al quale** (**alla quale, ai quali, alle quali**); **del quale; dal quale; nel quale; sul quale**:

La moglie del professore **alla quale** abbiamo telefonato è inglese.	*The wife of the teacher we telephoned is English.*

il cui, la cui, i cui, le cui (whose)

The form used depends on the gender and number of the object *not* on the person owning it:

Il ragazzo **le cui** pinne sono state rubate è inglese.	*The boy whose flippers were stolen is English.*

chi (he who, those who, etc.)

Chi is used in proverbs, generalisations and formal notices:

Chi non dorme piglia i pesci.	*The early bird catches the worm!* Lit: *He who doesn't sleep catches the fish*
Chi vuole venire in gita ad Assisi deve comprare il biglietto.	*Those who want to come on the excursion to Assisi must buy a ticket.*

In the last example, **chi** can be replaced by (**tutti**) **quelli che**, plural form and meaning:

Tutti quelli che vogliono venire ad Assisi devono comprare il biglietto.

Note these less common, more formal forms:

colui che, colei che, coloro che	*he who, she who, they who*

(tutto) ciò che, quello che (what, everything which)

These relatives do *not* refer to a specific thing or person:

Faccio **quello che** mi pare.	*I'll do as I please/what I like.*
Ciò che bisogna fare è parlargli subito.	*What we have to do is speak to him straightaway.*
Tutto quello che impari è utile.	*Everything you learn is useful.*
Prendi **tutto ciò che** vuoi.	*Take everything you want.*

il che (which)

Il che refers back to a *whole* clause or part of sentence:

Mi ha portato dei fiori, **il che** mi ha fatto molto piacere.	*He brought me some flowers, which made me very happy.*

8 Prepositions

8.1 a, di, da, in, per, con, su, tra, fra,

a

a) *To, at, in*:

a scuola	*(at school)*	a casa	*(at home)*
a letto	*(in bed)*	al mare	*(at the seaside)*

b) *Directions and distance*:

a destra, a sinistra	*on the right, on the left*
a nord, a sud (etc.)	*North, South (etc.)*
a dieci chilometri	*ten kms. away*
ad un'ora di strada	*an hour's drive away*

c) *Times and seasons*:

A Natale, a Pasqua	*at Christmas, at Easter*
a domani!	*(see you) tomorrow!*
alle cinque, a mezzogiorno	*at five o'clock, at midday*
un pasto al giorno	*one meal a day*

d) *Manner in which things are prepared*:

pollo allo spiedo	*chicken on the spit*
fatto a mano	*handmade*

e) *After certain adjectives or participles*:

pronto a	*ready to*
disposto a	*prepared to*

f) *Some prepositions require **a** with them*:

accanto a	*besides, next to*	davanti a	*in front of*
fino a	*as far as, until*	in capo a	*at the head/top of*
in cima a	*at the top of*	incontro a	*towards, against*
in fondo a	*at the bottom of*	di fronte a	*opposite*
in mezzo a	*in the middle of*	insieme a	*together with*
intorno a	*around*	quanto a	*as regards*
riguardo a	*on the subject of, as regards*		
rispetto a	*in comparison with, regarding*		
vicino a	*near*		

di

a) *Possession, belonging, etc.*:

la regina d'Inghilterra	*the Queen of England*
un film di Fellini	*a film by Fellini*

b) *Quantity, age, time (etc.)*:

un litro di vino	*a litre of wine*
un bambino di dieci anni	*a child of age ten*

c) *Composition and origin*:

un bicchiere di cristallo	*a crystal glass*
una signora di Firenze	*a lady from Florence*

d) *Time, seasons*:

d'inverno, di primavera	*in winter, in spring*
di mattina, di notte	*in the morning, at night*

e) *After certain adjectives and verbs*:

Sono stufo del lavoro.	*I'm bored with work.*
riempire di acqua	*to fill with water*

f) *Used as an adverb of manner*:

di nascosto	*hidden, by stealth*
di corsa	*in a hurry, at a rush*

g) *After **qualcosa, niente**:*

Non c'è niente di speciale.	*There's nothing special.*
Hai fatto qualcosa di bello?	*Have you done anything nice?*

h) *With prepositions that require* **di**:

a causa di	*because of*		
al di là di	*beyond (literally and figuratively)*		
fuori di	*outside*	invece di	*instead of*
per mezzo di	*by means of*	prima di	*before*

The pronouns listed below are usually followed by **di** only before pronouns such as **me, te, lui, lei** etc. Where there is a choice between **a** and **di**, the less common of the two is shown in brackets:

contro il muro *(against the wall)*	contro di noi *(against us)*
dietro il muro *(behind the wall)*	dietro di (a) me *(behind me)*
dentro l'armadio *(inside the cupboard)*	dentro di (a) me *(inside myself)*
dopo la tempesta *(after the storm)*	dopo di te *(after you)*
fra/tra amici *(between friends)*	fra di noi *(between ourselves)*
senza soldi *(without money)*	senza di te *(without you)*
sopra le nuvole *(above the clouds)*	sopra di (a) noi *(above us)*
sotto il letto *(under the bed)*	sotto a lui *(underneath him)*
sullo scaffale *(on the bookshelves)*	su di noi *(over us)*
verso casa *(towards home)*	verso di loro *(towards them)*

da

a) *By, from*:

È stato riparato dall'idraulico.	*It was repaired by the plumber.*
Il treno in arrivo da Pisa.	*The train arriving from Pisa.*

b) *Measurement, quantity, capacity, denomination*:

un francobollo da seicento lire	*a six-hundred-lire stamp*

c) *At the house/shop/restaurant of*:

Andiamo da Giovanni.	*We're going to Giovanni's.*
Vado dal medico.	*I'm going to the doctor's.*

d) *Physical characteristics*:

una signora dai capelli neri	*a woman with black hair*

e) *Joining* **molto, poco, niente, qualcosa** *to the infinitive*:

C'è poco da mangiare.	*There's not much to eat.*

f) *Indicating manner*:

Si è comportato da pazzo.	*He behaved like a madman.*
Sono andati da soli.	*They went by themselves.*

g) *Purpose*:

una camera da letto	*a bedroom*
un costume da bagno	*a bathing costume*

in

a) *Transport*:

in bicicletta, in aereo	*by bike, by plane*
in treno, in macchina	*by train, by car*

b) *Seasons*:

in primavera, in autunno	*in spring, in autumn*

c) *Other*:

Siamo in quattro.	*There are four of us.*
Se io fossi in te …	*If I were you …*
in orario, in ritardo	*on time, late*
in anticipo	*in advance, early*

d) *Dates*:

Mio figlio è nato nel 1979.	*My son was born in 1979.*

per

a) *For*:

I fiori sono per te.	*The flowers are for you.*

b) *Duration of time*:

Siamo qui per dieci giorni.	*We are here for ten days.*

c) *For (destination)*:

Sono partiti per la Francia.	*They've left for France.*

d) *Place*:

Ha buttato la giacca per terra.	*He threw the jacket on the ground.*
Giravano per le strade.	*They were wandering around the streets.*
Scendiamo per le scale.	*Let's go down the stairs.*

e) *Means of transport*:

Non mandare i soldi per posta.	*Don't send money by post.*
Puoi ringraziarla per telefono.	*You can thank her by phone.*

con

a) *With*:

Sono andata con Franco.	*I went with Franco.*

b) *Manner*:

con mia grande sorpresa	*to my great surprise*

c) *In expressions or phrases*:

E con questo?	*And so what?*

su

a) *On or onto*:

I bambini sono saltati sul muro.	*The children jumped onto the wall.*

b) *Out of*:

Tre gatti su cinque preferiscono il pesce.	*Three out of five cats prefer fish.*

c) *About, on a subject or topic*:

Ha parlato sul problema della droga.	*He spoke on the problem of drugs.*

d) *Expressions or phrases*:

sul giornale, sulla rivista	*in the newspaper, magazine*
un signore sui cinquanta anni	*a man of around fifty*
sul serio	*seriously*
su misura	*made to measure*

fra, tra

a) *Between or among*:

La casa è situata tra/fra la ferrovia e la superstrada.	*The house is situated between the railway line and the main road.*

b) *In, within (time)*:

Ci vediamo tra un'ora.	*See you in one hour.*

8.2 Combined preposition and article

The prepositions **a, da, in, su, d**i combine with **il, la, lo**, etc. to form **al, dal, nel, sul** (unit 4), and **del** (unit 10). It is rare for **con** or **per** to do this, but you may see the forms **col (con, il)** and **coi (con, i)**.

9 Negatives

In Italian a negative sentence must include **non** as well as a second negative word:

Non siamo **affatto** stanchi.	*We're not tired at all.*
Non siamo stanchi **per niente**.	*We're not tired at all.*
Non viene **nemmeno (neppure)** Luisa.	*Luisa's not coming either.*
Non c'è **nulla** da fare.	*There's nothing to be done.*
Non mi piacciono **né** Mara **né** suo marito.	*I don't like either Mara or her husband.*
Non ci vengo **più**.	*I'm not coming any more / any longer.*

Non comes before the verb, while the other negative comes after:

Preferisce **non** vederlo **più**.	*She prefers not to see him again.*
Non fate **più** queste cose!	*Don't do these things any more!*

In the case of the *passato prossimo*, the negative can also come in between **avere** and the participle (**mangiato**, etc):

Non ho **ancora** mangiato.	*I haven't eaten yet.*
or **Non** ho mangiato **ancora**.	
Non è **più** venuto.	*He didn't come any more.*
or **Non** è venuto **più**.	

The negatives **nulla, niente, nessuno, per niente, alcun, né ... né** come *after* the participle:

Non ho visto **nessuno**.	*I haven't seen anyone.*
Non mi è piaciuto per **niente**.	*I didn't like it at all.*

You can use two or even three negative expressions in one sentence:

Non ci vengo **mai più**.	*I'm not coming here ever again.*
Non mi regala **più niente**.	*He doesn't give me anything any more.*

Non ho **mai** detto **niente a nessuno**. *I've never told anyone anything.*

The negatives **nessuno, niente** or **nulla, mai, né...né, nemmeno, neppure, neanche** can all be placed at the beginning of the sentence, in which case the **non** is not needed. However – with the exception of **nessuno** – this reversed word order sounds less natural and somewhat dramatic:

Nessuno viene alla festa.	*No-one's coming to the party.*
Niente succede in questa città.	*Nothing happens in this town.*
Mai in vita mia ho visto una cosa simile!	*Never in my life have I seen something like this.*

Most of the negatives can be used on their own:

Io non ci vado stasera.	*I'm not going this evening.*
Neanch'io.	*Me neither.*
Sei mai stata in Cina?	*Have you ever been to China?*
Mai!	*Never!*
Pensate di tornare a Nocera?	*Do you think you'll go back to Nocera?*
Mai più!	*Never again!*
Mai visto!	Never seen anything like it!

Note the following idiomatic use of negatives:

Credo di **no**.	*I don't think so.*
È arrivato **senza niente**.	*He arrived without anything.*

10 Question words

10.1 Used in direct and indirect questions

Many common question words are covered in the Units, for example **dove, quale**. Others are illustrated here.

Quando? (when?)

Quando can be used in questions:

Quando partite?	*When are you going away?*

It can also be used in indirect or reported questions or statements:

Non mi ha detto **quando** vuole venire.	*He hasn't told me when he wants to come.*

Che? (which, what?)

Che is usually found with a noun, as in **Che cosa**?

Che cosa vuoi?	*What do you want?*

Using it on its own is considered slightly less elegant:

Che fai?	*What are you doing?*

Che is often used as an adjective, replacing **quale**? (*which?*)

Che macchina hai?	*What car do you have?*

Perché? (why?)

Perché is used in direct questions:

Perché ti sei messa quel vestito?	*Why have you put on that dress?*

And in indirect questions and statements:

Dimmi **perché** sei andata al cinema con Marco.	*Tell me why you went to the cinema with Marco.*

Come? (how?)

With **stare** to ask how someone is:

Come sta, signora Rossi?	*How are you, signora Rossi?*

With **essere** to ask what someone or something is like:

Com'è Marco?	*What is Marco like?*
Marco è alto, bruno.	*Marco is tall, dark.*
Come sono le tagliatelle?	*What are the tagliatelle like?*
Sono salate.	*They're too salty.*

Come is abbreviated before **è** to form **Com'è**.

Note the expression **come mai** (meaning *how come?*):

Come mai sei venuto a piedi?	*How come you came on foot?*

10.2 Question words used in exclamations

Come, che, quanto can all be used in exclamations as well:

Quanto sei bello!	*How nice you look!*
Come sei stupido!	*How stupid you are!*
Che antipatico che sei!	*How horrible you are!*

Used as above, **quanto** does not change ending. But when it means *what a lot of* it must agree with the noun:

Quanti bambini!	*What a lot of children!*
Quanta roba hai comprato!	*What a lot of stuff you've bought!*

11 Conjunctions

Conjunctions join parts of a sentence together; the two simplest examples are **ma** *(but)* and **e** *(and)*:

Vorrei andare a Parigi **ma** non ho soldi.	*I would like to go to Paris but I haven't any money.*

11.1 Simple conjunctions

Other simple conjunctions are:

altrimenti	*otherwise*	invece	*on the other hand*
anche	*also*	neanche, neppure,	
anzi	*rather, on the contrary, in fact*	nemmeno	*not even*
		o, oppure	*or, or else*
cioè	*that is, in other words*	perciò, quindi, pertanto, dunque	*so, therefore*
infatti	*in fact, indeed*	però, tuttavia	*yet, however, nevertheless*
inoltre	*besides*		
insomma	*in short*	piuttosto	*rather*

E normally becomes **ed** when followed by a vowel, especially by **e**.

11.2 Conjunctions requiring subjunctive

Some conjunctions (for example **perché** meaning *in order to*, **benché**) are followed by the subjunctive. These are illustrated in unit 10.

11.3 Conjunctions not requiring the subjunctive

Examples of conjunctions which do *not* need the subjunctive are:

Connecting words

Words such as **che** *(that)* **come** *(how, like, as)*:

Hai visto **come** era vestita?	*Did you see how she was dressed?*
È così stupido **che** non capisce niente.	*He's so stupid that he doesn't understand anything.*

Words expressing cause

Words such as **perché** (meaning *because*), **poiché, giacché, siccome, dal momento che** *(since)*:

Dal momento che abbiamo solo venti minuti, non possiamo fare tutto.	*Since we have only twenty minutes, we can't do everything.*

Perché takes the subjunctive when it means *in order to*.

Words expressing time

Words such as **quando** *(when)*, **mentre** *(while)*, **dopo che** *(after)*, **ogni volta che** *(every time that)*, **da quando** *(since)*, **(non) appena** *(as soon as)*, **finché** *(as long as)*:

Resta **finché** vuoi.	*Stay as long as you like.*

Finché takes the subjunctive when it means *until* (see unit 19).

Words expressing consequence

Words such as **e così** *(and so)*, **al punto che** *(to such an extent that)*, **talmente ...che** *(so much so that)*:

Ero **talmente** stanca **che** non ci capivo più niente.	*I was so tired that I didn't understand anything.*

12 Linking parts of sentences

Take care not to translate English into Italian directly. It doesn't always work. Here are some examples of how Italian and English handle structures in different ways.

12.1 Gerund, infinitive or past infinitive?

For use of the gerund with **stare**, see unit 6. The English gerund -*ing* form is sometimes translated by an Italian **gerundio**, sometimes not. As a general rule, you should use the Italian **gerundio** when the English gerund has a preposition with it such as *as, by, if, when* or has a preposition implied.

Entrando nella stanza, ho visto un disordine totale.

*Coming into the room, I saw a total mess. (**As** I came into the room, I saw a total mess.)*

Studiando di più, sarai promosso.

*(**By**) studying more, you will pass. (**If** you study more, you will pass.)*

When no preposition is mentioned or implied, use the *infinitive* form:

Fumare fa male.

Smoking is bad for you.

The infinitive is also used after the expressions **prima di, invece di**:

Prima di **uscire**, ha chiuso tutte le finestre.

Before going out, she closed all the windows.

Invece di **guardare** la televisione, fai i compiti.

Instead of watching tv, do your homework.

With **dopo**, use the *past infinitive*:

Dopo **aver mangiato**, ha bevuto un digestivo.

After eating, he drank a digestive liqueur.

Dopo **essersi alzato** alle 5, aveva solo voglia di andare a letto.

Having got up at 5am, he just wanted to go to bed.

The gerund also has a past form, formed with the gerund of **avere** or **essere** and the past participle (**-ato,-ito,-uto**, etc.):

Avendo studiato poco, sapeva che sarebbe stato bocciato.

Having studied little, he knew he would fail.

Essendo nato da quelle parti, conosceva bene la zona.

Having been born around there, he knew the area well.

12.2 Connecting verb and infinitive: introduction

Often a sentence has two connected verbs; the first verb tells us who is carrying out the action (*I, you, he*) while the second is an infinitive (*to go, to do*).

Certain verbs are followed directly by the verb in the infinitive (see unit 8 **potere**). Other verbs, on the other hand, need to be connected by **di** or **a** or in another way. Below is a list of the most common combinations:

12.3 Verbs linked directly to the infinitive

Auxiliary verbs *dovere, potere, preferire, sapere, volere*:

Non **so** nuotare.	*I can't swim.*
Preferisci andare a piedi?	*Do you prefer to go on foot?*

Impersonal verbs and verb phrases

Impersonal verbs **bisogna, basta, conviene**:

Basta imparare!	*You only have to learn!*
Non **conviene** risparmiare.	*It's not worth saving.*

Impersonal verb phrases such as **è bello, è conveniente, è difficile, è essenziale, è facile, è impossibile, è necessario, è possibile**:

È facile imparare l'italiano!	*It's easy to learn Italian!*
Non **è necessario** prenotare.	*It's not necessary to book.*

12.4 Verbs linked by *di*

Verbs of ending, finishing

Verbs such as **finire, smettere**, etc:

Finisco di mangiare poi vengo.	*I'll just finish eating then I'll come.*
Smettete di urlare!	*Stop shouting!*

Phrases using *avere* and a noun

These include **aver bisogno, aver fretta, aver tempo, aver intenzione, aver paura, aver vergogna, aver voglia di**:

Ho bisogno di cambiarmi.	*I need to change.*
Hai tempo di parlarmi?	*Do you have time to speak to me?*

12.5 Verbs linked by *a*

Verbs of beginning, starting

Verbs including **cominciare, iniziare, imparare**:

Comincio a preparare il pranzo.	*I'll start preparing the meal.*

Oggi **impariamo a** fare le lasagne.   *Today we're learning how to make lasagne.*

12.6 Verbs involving more than one person

When we ask or order someone to do something, we often use a verb which needs one preposition to link it to the person, and another preposition to link it to the infinitive (the action you want that person to carry out). Most commonly, such verbs take **a** before the person and **di** or **a** before the verb. (See unit 20)

Chiedo al cameriere **di** portare il menù.   *I'll ask the waiter to bring the menu.*

Insegno ai bambini **a** nuotare.   *I'm teaching the children to swim.*

At the end of the Grammar appendix, there is a list of common verbs showing how they link with the infinitive and/or with a person other than the subject of the verb.

suggerire   **a qcn**   **di**   *to suggest to someone to*

12.7 *Far fare, lasciar fare* (getting something done)

Fare

Fare can be used with an infinitive (for example **entrare, scendere**) to express the idea of getting something done, or making someone do something.

The direct object of **fare** can be an *object*:

Faccio riparare la macchina.   *I have/get the car repaired.*

Or a *person*:

Faccio pagare Antonio.   *I get Antonio to pay.*

Lasciare

A similar construction is possible with **lasciare** (*to let, allow*):

Lascio passare la signora.   *I let the lady pass.*

Double object

Look what happens when there are *two* objects (Antonio *and* a coffee) involved:

Faccio pagare il caffè **ad** Antonio.   *I get Antonio to pay for the coffee.*

Now see what happens when we add a person to the first example shown:

Faccio riparare la macchina **al** meccanico.   *I get the car repaired by the mechanic.*

In both cases, the person is now linked to the verb by **a**.

A can be replaced by **da** (*by*):

Faccio pagare il caffè **da** Antonio.   *I get the coffee paid for by Antonio.*

Faccio riparare la macchina **dal** meccanico.   *get the car repaired by the mechanic.*

Pronouns

The person or object can be replaced by a pronoun. The examples above would become:

Lo faccio pagare.   *I get **him** to pay.*
La faccio riparare.   *I get **it** repaired.*

Both person and thing can be replaced by pronouns:

Glielo faccio pagare.   *I get **him** to pay (for) **it**.*
Gliela faccio riparare.   *I get **him** to repair **it**.*

Fare plus infinitive

Here are some common combinations of **fare** and infinitive:

far avere	*to let someone have something*
far entrare	*to show someone in*
far pagare	*to charge someone (for something)*
far uscire	*to show someone out*
far vedere	*to show someone*
far venire	*to get someone to come, to call someone out*

The **e** is generally missed off the end of **fare** before the infinitive.

13 Verb extra

13.1 *Passato remoto*

The *passato remoto* (historic past) tense is more common in written Italian, especially in literary texts. However it is fairly widely used, even in spoken conversation, in the south of Italy, in situations where northerners would use the *passato prossimo*. It is important for students to be able to recognise it at least. Here are the forms of the *passato remoto* for each verb group:

---

parlare *(to talk, speak)*

parl**ai**	parl**ammo**
parl**asti**	parl**aste**
parl**ò**	parl**arono**

---

vendere *(to sell)*

vend**ei**/vend**etti**	vend**emmo**
vend**esti**	vend**este**
vend**é**/vend**ette**	vend**erono**/vend**ettero**

---

dormire *(to sleep)*

dorm**ii**	dorm**immo**
dorm**isti**	dorm**iste**
dorm**ì**	dorm**irono**

There are exceptions to this pattern particularly amongst the **-ere** verbs; the irregular *passato remoto* usually follows an alternating pattern of short and long forms, for example:

---

leggere *(to read)*

less**i**	legg**emmo**
legg**esti**	legg**este**
less**e**	less**ero**

Common verbs which have an irregular *passato remoto* are shown in the verb tables, with the two alternating forms.

13.2 Verbs and verb links

Here is a list of common verbs showing how they link with the infinitive
and/or with a person other than the subject of the verb. Where the
construction involves another person (**chiedo a qualcuno di fare
qualcosa**) this is shown by the abbreviation **qcn. (qualcuno)**:

Verb	(person)	Preposition	
abituarsi		a	*to get used*
accettare		di	*to accept*
aiutare	qcn	a	*to help someone to*
amare			*to love*
ammettere		di	*to admit*
andare		a	*to go*
aspettare		di	*to wait*
aspettarsi		di	*to expect*
augurarsi		di	*to hope, wish*
bastare			*to be enough*
bisognare			*to be necessary*
cercare		di	*to try*
cessare		di	*to cease*
chiedere	a qcn	di	*to ask someone to*
comandare	a qcn	di	*to order someone to*
cominciare		a	*to begin*
consigliare	a qcn	di	*to advise someone to*
continuare		a	*to continue*
correre		a	*to run*
costringere	qcn	a	*to force someone to*
credere		di	*to believe, think*
decidere		di	*to decide*
decidersi		a	*to decide*
desiderare			*to desire, want*
dimenticare		di	*to forget*
dire	a qcn	di	*to tell someone to*
divertirsi		a	*to enjoy oneself*
domandare	a qcn	di	*to ask someone to*
dovere			*to have to*
fare	qcn		*to make someone*
fare a meno		di	*to do without*

fare meglio		a	*to do better*
fare presto		a	*to hasten to*
fermarsi		a	*to pause, stop*
fingere		di	*to pretend*
finire		di	*to finish*
forzare	qcn	a	*to force someone to*
imparare		a	*to learn*
impedire	a qcn	di	*to prevent someone from*
incoraggiare	qcn	a	*to encourage someone to*
iniziare		a	*to begin to*
insegnare	a qcn	a	*to teach someone to*
invitare	qcn	a	*to invite someone to*
lamentarsi		di	*to complain*
lasciare			*to let, allow*
mandare	qcn	a	*to send someone to*
meravigliarsi		di	*to wonder*
mettersi		a	*to start off*
obbligare	qcn	a	*to oblige someone to*
occorrere			*to be necessary*
offrire		di	*to offer*
ordinare	a qcn	di	*to order someone to*
passare		a	*to stop by*
pensare		a	*to think about*
pensare		di	*to think of, decide to*
permettere	a qcn	di	*to allow someone to*
persuadere	qcn	a	*to persuade someone to*
piacere			*to please*
potere			*to be able*
preferire			*to prefer*
pregare	qcn	di	*to beg someone to*
prepararsi		a	*to get ready*
provare		a	*to try*
ricordarsi		di	*to remember*
rifiutarsi		di	*to refuse*
rimanere		a	*to stay*
rinunciare		a	*to give up*
riprendere		a	*to resume*
riuscire		a	*to succeed*

sapere		di	*to know, learn*
sbrigarsi		a	*to hurry*
sentire			*to hear*
sentirsela		di	*to feel like*
servire		a	*to be useful for*
smettere		di	*to stop*
sognare		di	*to dream*
sperare		di	*to hope*
stancarsi		di	*to tire*
stare		a	*to stay*
stupirsi		di	*to be amazed*
temere		di	*to be afraid*
tentare		di	*to attempt*
tornare		a	*to return*
vedere			*to see*
venire		a	*to come*
vergognarsi		di	*to be ashamed of*
vietare	a qcn	di	*to forbid someone to/from*
volere			*to want*

13.3 Common irregular verbs

Only the irregular parts of verbs are given. The full verb pattern for each tense or mood is given in full in the appropriate section of the book. Where alternative forms are possible, these are shown in brackets. Verbs which sometimes or always take **essere** in the *passato prossimo* are asterisked.

accorgersi *(to notice, realise)*   *p.p.* **accorto(si)***
Passato remoto: mi accorsi, ti accorgesti (etc.)
Similar verbs: scorgere (etc.)

andare *(to go)*   *p.p.* **andato** *
Present: vado, vai, va, andiamo, andate, vanno
Present subj: vada (etc.) andiamo, andiate, vadano
Imperative: vai (va'), vada, andiamo, andate, vadano
Future: andrò (etc.)   *Conditional:*   andrei (etc.)

aprire *(to open)*   *p.p.* **aperto**
Passato remoto: aprii (apersi), apristi, (etc.)
Similar verbs: coprire *(to cover)*, scoprire *(to discover)*, (etc.)

avere *(to have)*   *p.p.* **avuto**
Present: ho, hai, ha, abbiamo, avete, hanno
Present subj: abbia (etc.) abbiamo, abbiate, abbiano
Imperative: abbi, abbia, abbiamo, abbiate, abbiano
Future: avrò (etc.)   *Conditional:*   avrei (etc.)
Passato remoto::   ebbi, avesti, (etc.)

bere *(to drink)*   *p.p.* **bevuto**
Most parts of **bere** are derived from its original form **bevere** and follow
the normal **-ere** pattern.
Passato remoto: bevvi (bevetti), bevesti, (etc.)
Future: berrò (etc.)   *Conditional:*   berrei (etc.)

cadere *(to fall) p.p.* **caduto*** (or **avere**)
Passato remoto: caddi, cadesti, (etc.)
Future: cadrò   *Conditional:*   cadrei (etc.)
Similar verbs: accadere *(to happen)*,
                           scadere *(to fall due, expire)*

chiedere *(to ask)*   *p.p.* **chiesto**
Passato remoto: chiesi, chiedesti (etc.)
Similar verbs: richiedere *(to request)*

chiudere *(to shut, close)*   *p.p.* **chiuso**
Passato remoto: chiusi, chiudesti, (etc.)
Similar verbs: rinchiudere *(to shut in)*, schiudere *(to disclose)*

cogliere *(to gather, take)*   *p.p.* **colto**
Present: colgo, cogli, coglie, cogliamo, cogliete, colgono
Present subj: colga, cogliamo, cogliate, colgano
Imperative: cogli, colga, cogliamo, cogliete, colgano
Passato remoto: colsi, cogliesti (etc.)
Similar verbs: raccogliere *(to gather, collect)*,
                           accogliere *(to welcome)*, scogliere *(to dissolve)*

conoscere *(to get to know, meet)*   *p.p.* **conosciuto**
Passato remoto: conobbi, conoscesti, (etc.)
Similar verbs: riconoscere

correre *(to run)* p.p. **corso***
Passato remoto: corsi, corresti, (etc.)
Similar verbs: occorrere, percorrere, rincorrere, scorrere, (etc.)

crescere *(to grow)* p.p. **cresciuto*** (sometimes)
Passato remoto: crebbi, crescesti, (etc.)
Similar verbs: accrescere *(to increase)*, rincrescere *(to regret)*

dare *(to give)* p.p. **dato**
Present: do, dai, dà, diamo, date, danno
Present subj: dia, diamo, diate, diano
Imperative: da' (dai, dà), dia, diamo, date, diano
Passato remoto: diedi (detti), desti, diede (dette), demmo, deste, diedero (dettero)
Future: darò (etc.)
Conditional: darei (etc.)
Imperfect: davo (etc.)
Imperfect subj: dessi, dessi, desse, dessimo, deste, dessero
Similar verbs: ridare *(to give back)*

decidere *(to give back)* p.p. **deciso**
Passato remoto: decisi, decidesti, (etc.)

difendere *(to defend)* p.p. **difeso**
Passato remoto:: difesi, difendesti, (etc.)
Similar verbs: offendere *(to offend)*

dire *(to say)* p.p. **detto**
Present: dico, dici, dice, diciamo, dite, dicono
Present subj: dica, diciamo, diciate, dicano
Imperative: di', dica, diciamo, dite, dicano
Passato remoto: dissi, dicesti, etc.
Imperfect: dicevo (etc.)
Future: dirò (etc.) *Conditional:* direi (etc.)
Similar verbs: benedire, maledire, contraddire

discutere *(to discuss)* p.p. **discusso**
Passato remoto: discussi (discutei), discutesti, (etc.)

dividere *(to divide)* p.p. **diviso**
Passato remoto: divisi, dividesti, (etc.)

dovere *(to have to, to owe)*   *p.p.* **dovuto**

Present:	devo (debbo), devi, deve, dobbiamo, dovete, devono (debbono)
Present subj:	deva (debba), dobbiamo, dobbiate, devano (debbano)
Future:	dovrò (etc.)
Conditional:	dovrei (etc.)

essere *(to be)*   *p.p.* **stato***

Present:	sono, sei, è, siamo, siete, sono
Present subj:	sia (etc.), siamo, siate, siano
Imperative:	sii, sia, siamo, siate, siano
Future:	sarò (etc.) *Conditional:* sarei (etc.)
Passato remoto:	fui, fosti, fu, fummo, foste, furono
Imperfect:	ero, eri, era, eravamo, eravate, erano
Imperfect subj:	fossi, foste, fosse, fossimo, foste, fossero

fare *(to make, to do)*   *p.p.* **fatto**

Present:	faccio, fai, fa, facciamo, fate, fanno
Present subj:	faccia, facciamo, facciate, facciano
Imperative:	fa (fai, fa') faccia, facciamo, fate, facciano
Imperfect:	facevo
Imperfect subj:	facessi (etc.)
Future:	farò (etc.) *Conditional:* farei (etc.)
Passato remoto:	feci, facesti, (etc.)

giungere *(to reach, to arrive)*   *p.p.* **giunto***

Passato remoto:	giunsi, giungesti, (etc.)
Similar:	aggiungere, raggiungere, soggiungere

leggere *(to read)*   *p.p.* **letto**

Passato remoto:	lessi, leggesti, (etc.)
Similar verbs:	reggere, correggere, proteggere

mettere *(to put)*   *p.p.* **messo**

Passato remoto:	misi, mettesti, (etc.)
Similar verbs:	ammettere, scommettere, smettere, trasmettere

nascere *(to be born)*   *p.p.* **nato***

Passato remoto:	nacqui, nascesti, (etc.)
Similar verbs:	rinascere

nascondere *(to hide)*   *p.p.* **nascosto**
Passato remoto: nascosi, nascondesti, (etc.)

offrire *(to offer)*   *p.p.* **offerto**
Passato remoto: offrii (offersi), offristi, (etc.)
Similar verbs: soffrire *(to suffer)*

parere *(to appear)*   *p.p.* **parso***
Present: paio, pari, pare, pariamo (paiamo), parete, paiono
Present subj: paia, pariamo, pariate (paiate), paiano
Passato remoto: parvi, paresti, (etc.)
Future: parrò (etc.)   *Conditional:*   parrei (etc.)
Commonly found used impersonally: **mi pare** *(it seems to me)*

perdere *(to lose)*   *p.p.* **perduto/perso**
Passato remoto: persi (perdei, perdetti), perdesti, (etc.)

persuadere *(to persuade, convince)*   *p.p.* **persuaso**
Passato remoto: persuasi, persuadesti, (etc.)

piacere *(to please)*   *p.p.* **piaciuto***
Present: piaccio, piaci, piace, piacciamo, piacete, piacciono
Present subj: piaccia (etc.)
Passato remoto: piacque, piacesti, (etc.)
Similar verbs: compiacere, dispiacere

piangere *(to cry, weep)*   *p.p.* **pianto**
Passato remoto: piansi, piangesti, (etc.)
Similar verbs: compiangere, rimpiangere

piovere *(to rain (Incomplete verb))*   *p.p.* **piovuto*** (optional)
Passato remoto: piovve

porre *(to place, put)*   *p.p.* **posto**
(The parts of **porre** are derived from its original form **ponere**.)
Present: pongo, poni, pone, poniamo, ponete, pongono
Present subj: ponga, poniamo, poniate, pongano
Imperative: poni, ponga, poniamo, ponete, pongano
Passato remoto: posi, ponesti, (etc.)
Future: porrò (etc.)   *Conditional:*   porrei (etc.)
Imperfect: ponevo   *Imperfect subj:*   ponessi
Similar verbs: disporre, esporre, opporre, proporre, supporre

potere *(to be able to)* *p.p.* **potuto**
Present:	posso, puoi, può, possiamo, potete, possono
Present subj:	possa, possiamo, possiate, possano
Future:	potrò (etc.) *Conditional:* potrei (etc.)
Passato remoto:	potei (potetti), potesti, (etc.)

prendere *(to take)* *p.p.* **preso**
Passato remoto:	presi, prendesti, (etc.)

ridere *(to laugh)* *p.p.* **riso**
Passato remoto:	risi, ridesti, (etc.)

rimanere *(to remain, stay)* *p.p.* **rimasto***
Present:	rimango, rimani, rimane, rimaniamo, rimanete, rimangono
Present subj:	rimanga, rimaniamo, rimaniate, rimangano
Imperative:	rimani, rimanga, rimaniamo, rimanete, rimangano
Passato remoto:	rimasi, rimanesti, (etc.)
Future:	rimarrò (etc.) *Conditional:* rimarrei (etc.)

rispondere *(to reply)* *p.p.* **risposto**
Passato remoto:	risposi, rispondesti, (etc.)
Similar verbs:	corrispondere

rompere *(to break)* *p.p.* **rotto**
Passato remoto:	ruppi, rompesti, (etc.)
Similar verbs:	corrompere, interrompere

salire *(to go up, climb up)* *p.p.* **salito***
Present:	salgo, sali, sale, saliamo, salite, salgono
Present subj:	salga, saliamo, saliate, salgano
Imperative:	sali, salga, saliamo, salite, salgano

sapere *(to know, learn a fact)* *p.p.* **saputo**
Present:	so, sai, sa, sappiamo, sapete, sanno
Present subj:	sappia, sappiamo, sappiate, sappiano
Imperative:	sappi, sappia, sappiamo, sapete, sappiano
Future:	saprò (etc.) *Conditional:* saprei (etc.)
Passato remoto:	seppi, sapesti, (etc.)

scegliere *(to choose)* *p.p.* **scelto**
Present:	scelgo, scegli, sceglie, scegliamo, scegliete, scelgono
Present subj:	scelga, scegliamo, scegliate, scelgano

Imperative:	scegli, scelga, scegliamo, scegliete, scelgano
Passato remoto:	scelsi, scegliesti, (etc.)

scendere *(to descend, get down)* *p.p.* **sceso***
Passato remoto:	scesi, scendesti, (etc.)
Similar verbs:	ascendere

scrivere *(to write)* *p.p.* **scritto**
Passato remoto:	scrissi, scrivesti, (etc.)

sedere *(to sit)* *p.p.* **seduto**
Present:	siedo, siedi, siede, sediamo, sedete, siedono
Present subj:	sieda (segga), sediamo, sediate, siedano (seggano)
Imperative:	siedi, sieda, sediamo, sedete, siedano
Note reflexive form:	

sedersi *(to sit (down))* *p.p.* **seduto(si)***

stare *(to be, stay, stand)* *p.p.* **stato***
Present:	sto, stai, sta, stiamo, state, stanno
Present subj:	stia, stiamo, stiate, stiano
Imperative:	sta (stai, sta'), stia, stiamo, state, stiano
Passato remoto:	stetti, stesti, (etc.)
Imperfect:	stavo (etc.)
Imperfect subj:	stessi, stessi, stesse, stessimo, steste, stessero

tenere *(to hold)* *p.p.* **tenuto**
Present:	tengo, tieni, tiene, teniamo, tenete, tengono
Present subj:	tenga, teniamo, teniate, tengano
Imperative:	tieni, tenga, teniamo, tenete, tengano
Future:	terrò (etc.) *Conditional:* terrei (etc.)
Passato remoto:	tenni, tenesti, (etc.)
Similar verbs:	appartenere, contenere, mantenere, ritenere, sostenere, trattenere

togliere *(to take away, take off)*: see **cogliere**

uscire *(to go out)* *p.p.* **uscito***
Present:	esco, esci, esce, usciamo, uscite, escono
Present subj:	esca, usciamo, usciate, escano
Imperative:	esci, esca, usciamo, uscite, escano
Similar verbs:	riuscire (to succeed)

vedere *(to see)* *p.p.* **visto/veduto**
Passato remoto: vidi, vedesti, (etc.)
Future: vedrò (etc.)   *Conditional:*   vedrei (etc.)

venire *(to come)* *p.p.* **venuto***
Present: vengo, vieni, viene, veniamo, venite, vengono
Present subj: venga, veniamo, veniate, vengano
Imperative: vieni, venga, veniamo, venite, vengano
Future: verrò (etc.)   *Conditional:*   verrei (etc.)
Passato remoto: venni, venisti, etc.
Similar verbs: avvenire, convenire, divenire, svenire

vivere *(to live)* *p.p.* **vissuto*** (optional)
Passato remoto: vissi, vivesti, (etc.)
Future: vivrò (etc.)   *Conditional:*   vivrei (etc.)

volere *(to want to)* *p.p.* **voluto**
Present: voglio, vuoi, vuole, vogliamo, volete, vogliono
Present subj: voglia, vogliamo, vogliate, vogliano
Future: vorrò (etc.)   *Conditional:*   vorrei (etc.)
Passato remoto: volli, volesti, (etc.)

INDEX

Note: The numbers refer to units not pages; numbers preceded by G refer to Grammar appendix. For details of functions covered, see also the contents list.